# Market Incentives to End War

# Market Incentives to End War

◆

## Conflict Reduction Bonds

*Ronnie Horesh*

iUniverse, Inc.

New York  Lincoln  Shanghai

# Market Incentives to End War
## Conflict Reduction Bonds

iUniverse, Inc.

For information address:
iUniverse, Inc.
2021 Pine Lake Road, Suite 100
Lincoln, NE 68512
www.iuniverse.com

ISBN: 0-595-29484-7

# Contents

# Introduction, the scale of the problem

We are, understandably, not quite rational about war. We regard its opposite, peace, as an ideal: as unattainable as it is desirable; something to be worshipped from afar, and something that will never actually happen. War appears to many of us, as it did to the ancient Greeks, to be part of the natural order of things.

This book is different. It assumes nothing about either the inevitability of conflict, or its causes. It will take as its starting point only the reality of conflict. It will not assume that the idealists and ideologues, the politicians, the generals, and the men of religion are the best people to bring peace to the world, but neither will it assume that none of them have any contribution to make. It will propose not a single way of ending violent political conflict, but rather a way of stimulating solutions to war that does not prejudge its causes. It will introduce a new financial instrument designed, in effect, to contract out to whoever is most capable, the achievement of peace.

This author sees violent political conflict as amenable to real world solutions. We do not need to know the exact nature of these solutions in advance, but we can put in place a mechanism that will encourage and reward people for finding them. Conflict Reduction Bonds aim to bridge the gap between our everyday political environment and the seemingly remote ideal of a world without war.

In the single year 2000 war directly killed 310 000 people; about 0.56 percent of all world deaths. But this figure massively understates the suffering wars cause.[1] Indirectly, armed political conflict kills many more.[2] In the 1990s 3.6 million people, most of them civilians, were killed in conflict.[3] In the entire 20th century, an estimated 191 million people lost their lives directly or indirectly as a result of conflict—and well over half of them were civilians.[4] This amounts to about one in 22, or 4.5 per cent of all human deaths during that century. (Rough calculations suggest that this is a higher proportion of deaths attributable to conflict than in the 19th century.[5]) In 2001 the United Nations High Commissioner for Refugees estimated that the UN was attempting to help 21.8 million refugees and internally displaced persons as the result of conflict.[6] Since the end of the Cold War, 90 per cent of those killed in conflict have been non-combatants, compared with 15 per cent at the beginning of the 20th century[7] and 65 per cent in World War II, including holocaust victims.[8]

And, of course, war also maims and sickens people.[9] [10] It destroys social fabrics and coping mechanisms. As well, resources devoted to the military or to peacekeeping are unavailable to the life-enhancing sectors of the world economy. Global military spending exceeds $800 billion every year—a colossal sum. War traumatises non-combatants, and fear of war, fed by the endless accounts of war worldwide, adds to people's anxiety, however distant they may be from current conflict. The possibility of war leads to underinvestment of people and resources in places that sorely need them. It accelerates the migration of blighted countries' best and brightest to stable countries, governed by law.

Neither do the trends, at first sight, appear encouraging. True, the end of the Cold War in 1990 has seen a sharp downward trend in such components of global warfare as ethnic rebellion,[11] forcibly dislocated populations,[12] and autocratic 'command' authority systems. The number and magnitude of armed conflicts within and between states have lessened since the early 1990s by nearly half.[13] These trends have been paralleled by upward trends in democracy: democratic governments now outnumber autocratic governments two to one and continue to be more successful than autocracies in resolving violent societal conflicts[14] [15]— and in settling conflicts.[16] Conflicts over self-determination are being settled with ever-greater frequency, usually when ethnic groups gain greater autonomy and power-sharing within existing states.[17]

But the world has not entered a new era of universal peace. Some researchers have reported a substantial increase in serious wars (i.e. wars with greater than 1000 battle-related deaths in a given year) in the latter 1990s. Others have made an even bolder claim: that the general downward trend in armed conflict has been reversed in the late 1990s.[18] New kinds of war are being fought that are less disciplined and more spontaneous than the old. It is in these 'low-intensity' wars, occurring in recent times in Ivory Coast, Somalia, Sudan, Liberia, East Timor and the former Yugoslavia, that the civilian proportion of the dead reaches 90 per cent.[19]

Meanwhile the *potential* for violent political conflict, represented by nuclear weapons proliferation, is increasing. The total world nuclear stockpile now consists of over 36 800 warheads. (In addition to deployed nuclear warheads, thousands more are held in reserve and are not counted in official declarations.[20]) As this is being written, in mid-2003, the leader of a poverty-stricken state, North Korea, has the capacity to threaten neighbouring countries with nuclear weapons.

So violent political conflict takes many diverse forms: from the piling up of atomic and nuclear weapons in failed states, to armed insurrections by nationalists in West Africa. Some authorities respond to these challenges with state terror, repression, and political mass murder. Economic growth, the dissemination of current technology, and research into new technology could mean that access to weapons of mass destruction will widen still further. Now it is not only nation states, but also well-funded and well-organised terrorist groups that have the capability to acquire and use, for example, atomic or chemical weapons. The need for new solutions to violent political conflict, as urgent as it is today, is fast becoming an absolute necessity.

War therefore is a major social, health and economic problem. Of course, it is not our only such problem—suicides claimed more than 815 000 lives in the year 2000, while the World Health Organisation estimates that there are around 300 million acute cases of malaria resulting in one million deaths every year.[21] Of all humankind's many troubles, however, war is perhaps the most disheartening because it is not a natural disaster or an unavoidable 'Act of God'; its casualties result from human beings' deliberate use of force on one another.

But if the twentieth century brought the steady advance of war, and an increase in the proportion of casualties accounted for by civilians, it also brought the beginnings of organised human resistance to war. Since everyone is now expected to participate in one way or another, or to become a victim whether they participate or not, opposition could develop to the institution of war itself, and not just to a warrior elite, which today takes the form of the chieftains of the military-industrial complex.[22]

It is worth briefly pointing out *why* ways of reducing conflict are suggested. Essentially it is because the 'costs' of conflict almost always outweigh the 'benefits'. The costs are to be interpreted broadly; they include, in no particular order, the negative humanitarian, social, economic, environmental and distributional impacts of violent political conflict. But there are benefits too, and they are not limited to those that flow directly from military spending. They also include the freedoms won from tyrannies deposed by conflict. There *are* instances, such as the war to defeat Hitler, where the benefits of waging a successful war are almost universally thought to outweigh the very grievous costs. It is arguable that any means of reducing conflict should not discourage wars that generate such net benefits. But it would also be far better to avoid the circumstances that precipitated 'necessary' or 'just' wars on violent regimes ever arising in the first place. These invariably comprise the use of force on populations either within or outside the regimes' borders.

Most people need no convincing that violent political conflict adds to the burden of human misery. These include especially the countless millions currently caught up in hostilities, who would like nothing more than to live their lives undisturbed by conflict. As well, it is safe to assume that a large proportion of those in governments, religious bodies, non-governmental organisations (NGOs), and other positions of authority also prefer peace to conflict. Tragically though, there are many in positions of power or influence who are half-hearted about peace; others who feel threatened by it, and others who, for whatever reason, actively promote violence. Conflict often serves the ends of a minority of actors, who may profit from the exploitation of resources such as timber, minerals, guns, and drugs, or the illegal trafficking in persons. The power of such individuals is enhanced by instability.[23] But this book will take as it as axiomatic that the 'benefits' from violent political conflict enjoyed by such individuals are outweighed by the costs imposed on the far more numerous victims, and that reducing conflict is a worthwhile end in itself.

This book is entirely focussed on that desired outcome. It will introduce a means of rewarding successful achievement of world peace, rather than activities that are supposedly aimed at achieving this goal. It will describe and explain a new financial instrument, Conflict Reduction Bonds, which will not be a single solution to war. Rather, their aim is to stimulate an array of solutions, each appropriate to the highly variable circumstances of particular conflicts.

Definitions of conflict are crucial, and will be discussed in more detail below. But, in general, 'violent political conflict' refers both to wars between different states and to domestic political conflict, while 'peace-building' and 'conflict reduction' or 'conflict minimisation' can be taken as synonymous.

Chapter 1 briefly surveys current conflicts and conflict-minimisation methods. Chapter 2 looks at the importance of markets and the targeting of outcomes, as possible pointers to a solution. Chapter 3 outlines how Conflict Reduction Bonds, the subject of this book, would work. Chapters 4 and 5 look, respectively, at the advantages and potential pitfalls of a bond regime. Chapter 6 looks at some practical aspects of a bond regime and chapter 7 is a summary and conclusion.

# 1

# *Preventing conflict*

The best way of reducing conflict is to preventing it from starting. This chapter looks at efforts to identify the root causes of conflict, and at current institutional attempts to prevent conflict.

## ROOT CAUSES

To those of us fortunate to be distant spectators of violent political conflict it all seems very simple. War between country A and country B is inevitable, we think, because they both want the same piece of land. Or the inhabitants of country A believe in X while the inhabitants of country B believe in Y. Or within country C the ruling party is of ethnic group D and rich, while the masses are of ethnic group E and poor. Once conflict is actually happening it is not difficult for outsiders to give plausible reasons for its occurrence, or even its inevitability.

Poverty, ignorance, despair, and differences of wealth, ethnicity, religion,[24] class, culture or ideology: all these are thought to be some of the 'root causes' of war and violence. So are inequalities in access to resources, scarcity and economic decline, insecurity, the violation of human rights, exclusion or persecution of sectoral groups, and state failures including declining institutional and political legitimacy and capacity. Other key foundations for conflict could be historical legacies, regional threats, the availability of weapons, economic shocks, and the extension or withdrawal of external support.[25] Large numbers of unemployed males may also catalyse conflict.

Inward factors are also cited; such as individual pathologies, like a history of being abused that predisposes someone to take up violence in later life. Often blamed too are the media, and the frequency with which our children are exposed to images of violence—especially when violence is presented as an acceptable and effective way of solving problems.

1

No doubt all these factors can and do play a part in fomenting and fanning the flames of conflict. But even aside from the impossibility of eliminating every potential cause of conflict, there is no *inevitability* that these causes will lead to war. Selective memory has strengthened these linkages in the collective mind, but for each of these 'root causes' there are examples that disprove any simple cause-and-effect relationship. There are dozens of countries in which people of different ethnicity and religion live happily side-by-side. There are also thousands of decent, peaceable and fulfilled adults who as children were horribly abused. One researcher into child abuse concluded that it does increase the risk of later criminality—but not always. The 'intergenerational transmission of violence is not inevitable,' she wrote.[26] There are many instances of land disputes that have ended. Take, for example, the border between Scotland and England, once the setting of a 300-year old series of bloody conflicts, now as peaceful as any border in the world. The Swiss have a high rate of gun ownership and an enviable absence of internal political conflict, as well as a low rate of gun crime. Japan is still a relatively peaceful society, but one in which lurid depictions of violence are avidly produced, promulgated and consumed, and have been for many years. Paul Collier and the World Bank, examining the world's civil wars since 1960, concluded that although tribalism is often a factor it is rarely the main one. They also found that societies composed of several different ethnic and religious groups were actually less likely to experience civil war than homogeneous societies.[27]

It would seem likely, then, that political violence cannot be *inextricably* linked to one, or even several, root causes. What could be a root cause of conflict in one region can be irrelevant in another. Elimination of supposed root causes, such as poverty, could alleviate tension in one particular conflict, but it could conceivably by, say, allowing more to be spent on weapons, inflame conflict in another. Availability of small arms in most societies probably does inflame conflict: the low Swiss murder rate, for example, is underpinned by strict gun control laws. There is no formula connecting any alleged root cause with conflict such that removing it will always and inevitably lessen the chance of conflict.

As well, the factors that generate conflict may differ from those that make it feasible. In general, the existence of some form of grievance, whether economic, political, or social in nature, appears to be the most persuasive motivation for conflict. Economic motivations—whether the pursuit of resources for war-financing or for elite self-enrichment—appear more significant in sustaining, prolonging, and transforming conflict. The role of valuable natural resources is more ambivalent. They can make conflict more feasible when grievances already exist, as they offer a ready means of financing rebellion. But they can also become a source of grievance in themselves, if state institutions responsible for their management instead engage in corruption.[28] It is not always clear in which way is the direction of causation. In some cases, resource competition can exacerbate civil war. In others, civil war can exacerbate competition over resources.

Neither is it always clear which particular 'root causes' are operating even once a conflict has started. Explanations for the civil war in Lebanon from 1975-90 centred on ethnic or ideological causes of the conflict. But since the end of the conflict, economic developments, and rampant corruption in particular, seem to imply that economic opportunities were probably more important. The civil war resulted in the entry of new actors and an unprecedented rise in the level of social and political power, financial accumulation, and exercise of violence surrounding pre-existing, illegal drug-related activities. For local militias, drugs not only provided a means by which to pay wages, procure arms, and materiel, but also a source of capital accumulation among their leaders and middlemen. This trade resulted in trans-communal, regional cooperation between producers and militias, who negotiated the division of labour and took a share of the profits. These groups, therefore, had a collective interest in prolonging the war. The authorities have since done little to dismantle the drug networks and their factories. As a result, there has been long-term integration of these networks into the international drug market. Satisfaction of 'greed' in the name of 'creed' would have been impossible if not for cooperation across allegedly 'intractable' communal boundaries.[29]

These findings echo the pioneering work of Lewis Fry Richardson, who gathered data on all the wars of recent times, that is from 1820 to 1949. Rather than ranking wars by historical importance, or by relevance to later events, he picked the most objective measure he could find: the number killed, and focussed on those conflicts that killed more than 3000, for which the data were reasonably complete. There were 108 such conflicts during the 130-year period of study described in his seminal *Statistics of Deadly Quarrels*.[30] World Wars I and II together accounted for some 36 million deaths, or about 60 per cent of all the deaths of his study period. (This total excludes those caused by famine and disease associated with war.[31]) While compiling his list of wars, Richardson noted the various items that historians mentioned as possible irritants or pacifying influences, and then he looked for correlations between these factors and belligerence. The results were almost uniformly disappointing. There were tendencies or correlations, but no unambiguous causal relationships. So states tended to become involved in wars in proportion to the number of states with which they have common frontiers, though in proportion to their possible contacts for war-making, sea powers seem to have been less belligerent than land powers. Richardson's own suppositions about the importance of arms races were not confirmed; he found evidence of a preparatory arms race in only 13 out of 315 cases. Richardson was also a proponent of Esperanto, but found that similarity and difference of language appeared to have little influence on the occurrence of wars, contrary to the belief of some advocates of universal languages. Economic indicators were equally unhelpful: economic causes seem to have featured directly in fewer than 29 per cent of the wars since between 1820 and 1949. The statistics neither confirm nor refute the ideas that war is mainly a struggle between the rich and the poor or that commerce between nations creates bonds that prevent war.[32]

So it is not always obvious, even after a long conflict has ended, what its 'root causes' were, and perhaps the very notion of a 'root cause' needs questioning. It implies that factors such as 'poverty' or 'ethnicity' can be removed from their social context, and somehow dealt with, and that then a desired result will follow. But human societies are complex. Poverty can feed grievance, but grievance can be a result of poverty. No single formula, no single set of parameters will always lead to conflict, and guarantee freedom from conflict. Indeed, even the notion of 'causation' in this context is questionable. Perhaps we should leave the last word to Tolstoy:

> The deeper we delve in search of these causes the more of them we discover, and each single cause or series of causes appears to us equally valid in itself, and equally false by its insignificance compared to the magnitude of the event.[33]

## CONFLICT PREVENTION

If the intellectual underpinning of a root causes approach is fragile, so too is the institutional structure that exists to prevent conflict. And just as generals are often accused of fighting the battles of the last war, so too have many of the organisations trying to prevent conflict been slow to adapt to the post-Cold War environment.

Resources devoted to conflict resolution have recently begun shifting toward conflict prevention and away from containing, mitigating and terminating active conflicts.[34] Conflict prevention aims to deter conflicts and crises before they escalate: it comes into play early in a conflict and address some of conflict's causes, building early warning and other institutional capacities to anticipate and cope with conflicts early on. These new methods to anticipate and keep incipient conflicts from erupting have joined older techniques of managing and resolving exist-ing conflicts.[35]

The United Nations has been criticised for institutional weakness and inflexi-bility in this area. There is no single UN agency responsible for conflict preven-tion. The Secretary-General has designated the Department of Political Affairs the focal point for conflict prevention initiatives, but numerous other depart-ments, funds, and agencies are also engaged in preventive work. Coordination and mainstreaming of prevention is thus important. Recent reforms have helped raise the profile of prevention and improved the quality and effective transmis-sion of relevant data and analysis throughout the UN system. But it is accepted that, since prevention can often seem to be everyone's business, it may, at times, seem to fall at no one's door.[36]

Perhaps the single official whose mandate is solely conflict prevention is the Organization for Security and Co-operation in Europe's High Commissioner on National Minorities, and his charge allows him to act only in pre-crisis situations; if they heat up, he must disengage. Another example: the UN High Commis-sioner for Refugees can only alleviate refugees' plight, not address the forces that caused it. More fundamental criticisms concern the structure of the UN Security Council, set up 50 years ago, in a world in which there were several powers in the top tier. To make the system workable all were given a veto. Today's world has but one such power, the United States, and the old structure is seen by some as inappropriate and dangerously irrelevant. And the Security Council, though technically empowered to act on threats to international peace and security that arise within member countries, has mainly concerned itself with inter-state con-flicts. Yet the 15 most deadly conflicts in, for example, 2001—those that killed over 100 people—were all intra-state conflicts, but all of them were directly affected by external actors and 11 of them spilled over international borders. Eleven of the conflicts have lasted for eight or more years.[37]

Many overseas aid programmes have, as an implicit objective, conflict preven-tion. But few donors exert the leverage that they could. In fact, development assistance can even, inadvertently, contribute to conflict. There are some difficult questions, that need a flexible, pragmatic and most importantly, peace-orientated approach to answer Mechanisms should evaluate the effects of aid on the proba-bility of its increasing the likelihood of conflict. How benefits from aid projects are controlled and distributed might well aggravate conflict. Is western-style democracy likely to increase conflict? What about rapid economic development and globalisation? It might make economic sense to help finance a port, a road or a dam. But these facilities can enhance a national or local tyrant's position, and make aggression more viable.

Government agencies and international organisations concerned with conflict are still mainly geared towards dealing with conflict once it has become violent, rather than preventing it arising in the first place. Too often in today's world the international community becomes involved in such conflict-prevention activities as mediation and peacekeeping only when the protagonists are facing each other or have actually begun armed conflict. There is also some institutional reluctance to become involved. Many development professionals, for example, see the more immediate causes of national conflicts as 'getting into politics' and thus something that should be left to military agencies,[38] or as interference in a country's internal affairs. There have been positive moves. The international community has put increasing emphasis on preventing conflicts, and on containing conflicts that have already broken out.[39]

Many international agencies, especially those created during the Cold War, have discrete 'specific and defined sets of problems', and concern themselves with issues such as arms control, development, security assistance, health, or agriculture. Their distinct functions often mean that these agencies work in isolation from each other and sometimes at cross-purposes. One agency may be trying to prevent violent conflicts, while another (or another part of the same agency) may be doing things that aggravate them. There have been recent examples of aid being used to fuel conflict, or of the intent of trade sanctions being subverted, so that a repressive regime is the main beneficiary.[40]

There is a strong case for subordinating all aspects of development programs into coherent, effective anti-conflict strategies. It is simply made: violent political conflict can quickly wipe out any development gains. There should be built-in incentives for aid donors to consider these issues.

Research suggests, for example, that conflict could be mitigated by diverting foreign aid in an armed conflict area to those countries contiguous to a civil war, especially those with longer common borders, since these are most prone to civil-war spillovers.[41] Objective criteria could be developed for the authorization or refusal of arms exports had been developed. Governments could authorise or refuse arms exports applications by reference to factors such as the occurrence of armed conflicts, a state's human rights record and its level of militarization.[42] There is a strong case too, for trying innovative policies, some of which cannot effectively be performed by government, or government-funded agencies. These could include subsidising of anti-hate broadcasts, or trust-building measures which, because of their very nature, are viewed with suspicion when undertaken by officially approved bodies.

## DISCUSSION

In all these areas, there should be incentives for organisations and their staff to act preventively, which may mean going beyond traditional job descriptions. Aid organisations, such as international or domestic NGOs monitoring human rights, and others should be encouraged to monitor countries' domestic behaviour and to alert the world community to possible violent conflicts, repression or dispersion of nuclear technology. But it is too easy, and not especially helpful, to use words like 'flexibility', 'pragmatic', and to utter platitudes like 'address root causes when appropriate', or 'increase co-ordination between agencies'. This author takes no pleasure in repeating these mantras, and believes that more flexibility, pragmatism, interdisciplinary communication, or whatever, is not necessarily better. Rather, there is probably an optimal level of each of these qualities, and there is no evidence that we are not at that optimal level, whether in efforts to prevent conflict or in any of the other ways of resolving or mitigating conflict. Unfortunately, though, neither is there any evidence that we now have optimal levels of flexibility, etc.

Public choice theory would have it that international peacekeeping organisations are inherently cynical, in the sense that their overriding interest is to perpetuate their own existence. The truth is, we do not know whether these organisations are effective, ineffective, or even counter-effective in minimising conflict. Still less do we know whether they are efficient, in terms of achieving a worthwhile reduction in conflict per unit dollar outlay. Most probably, their performance varies, though it is likely their existence as fora within which people from different countries interact, however ineffectually, serves a positive purpose, most of the time. One problem these organisations suffer from is lack of resources—at least in comparison with those who profit from conflict. Unfortunately there is no definitive way of showing that more funding would bring about more peace, or that such funding would be the most cost-effective way of reducing conflict.

In short, there are no mechanisms in place to monitor, in an over-arching way, the distribution of conflict-reduction resources to make sure that they are achieving the best possible return for their outlay and nor are there incentives to set up such monitoring systems. The widespread presence of violent political conflict, the human cost of conflict, and the potential for further conflict; all suggest that it is worth investigating new approaches, even in the absence of definitive proof that anything new will work.

A second, and related problem though is that neither these organisations, nor the people that work for them, either permanently or on short-term contracts, are paid according to results. They have only indirect incentives to seek out and develop those ways of minimising conflict that are most cost-effective. They might even face disincentives to achieve their supposed objectives. This is not to say that these employees are especially lazy or incompetent. They behave rationally given the incentives they face, but these incentives do not consistently reward the achievement of desired outcomes. There is no question that the people who work for these organisations are competent and well-meaning. But however well-intentioned, neither these bodies, nor their agents, are rewarded in ways that correlate with its success in achieving peaceful resolution of political conflict.

Let us be clear what we are saying here. The individuals who work for these organisations are no doubt highly motivated and derive immense personal satisfaction from seeing their work translated into a reduced level of worldwide political conflict. No, lack of pecuniary incentives has two other dimensions. First, the funding of these bodies bears no relationship with their success or otherwise in reducing conflict. This means that the net resources at each organisation's command including the number of professional and support personnel, and non-labour resources, are unrelated to their efficiency or effectiveness in reducing conflict. Second, while there are well-intentioned and highly motivated people who work for these organisations without expecting (or wanting) high financial compensation, there are also others who would be more willing and able to work for these organisations, even on short-term contracts, if there were more funds available either for their compensation, or for expanding the range of resources at their disposal, which would make it easier for them to do their job effectively.

It is in this context that we need to consider the problem of lack of resources. Conflict prevention appears to be one poorly resourced area. Only a handful of agencies or programmes have explicitly added conflict prevention to their mandate, including the UN Secretariat. This may be because or a sense of fatalism: a sense that conflict is inevitable, so why bother trying to prevent it? But it may also be a result of the inefficiency of current conflict prevention methods. Since they are so ineffective, it is rational to channel limited resources into other areas, where they will bring about a better return. It follows that increasing efficiency, as measured by conflict-reduction per unit outlay would bring double benefits: the efficiencies would be valuable in their own right, but they would also lead to more resources being deployed to reduce conflict in the future.

Our quick look at root causes and conflict prevention makes clear that policies attempting to reduce conflict must be capable of adapting to diverse and changing circumstances. They must subordinate both their intellectual approach and any institutional structures to the reduction of conflict. In other words, the desired outcome should drive the policies and their funding, not the other way round.

# 2

# *Toward a solution: markets and outcomes*

The previous chapter touched on some of the difficulties of identifying causal relationships between conflict and its possible precursors and looked at some of the real-world institutional rigidities that bedevil conflict prevention. Similar complexities, of course, festoon the resolution of conflicts that are already in progress. All these difficulties point to the need for a rational, flexible and adaptive mechanism for allocating conflict-reduction resources. This chapter will argue that market forces should be used to stimulate appropriate resource allocation decisions. It will look at examples of ways in which government has tried to use different 'more market' approaches to solving domestic social problems.

## CONFLICT, MARKETS AND PLURALISM

Conflict reduction, when attempted by the United Nations and other bodies can be an explicit goal; or it can be one of the implicit goals of more general aid programmes. The resources for all conflict-reduction activities are, of course, limited. In economic theory, and on all the historical evidence, markets are the most efficient means yet discovered of allocating society's scarce resources. Unfortunately, many believe that market forces must inevitably conflict with social goals. Understandably so, since in recent decades deregulation of some economies and an enhanced role for markets have made many people very wealthy indeed, while the less well-off have gained relatively little and many social and environmental problems appear to have worsened.

So it is important to remind ourselves that market forces and self-interest can serve public, as well as private, goals. Often, these private goals coincide with social goals, so that, for instance, the market routinely performs vital tasks such as food distribution and the provision of such indispensables as home medicines, baby needs, furniture and other consumer goods. These are exceedingly complex tasks but, left to the multiplicity of agents operating in reasonably competitive markets, they are accomplished in ways that fulfil not only the private goals of the firms and consumers involved but also society's goal of efficient supply of goods and services. This feat results from the combination of the self-interest of large numbers of market players, and their ability to react appropriately to ever-changing circumstances. Some would attribute the triumph of the western market economies over the state-controlled, centrally-planned economies of the Soviet Union and its satellites to the victory of materialist motivations over political ideals. But it is more likely that the efficiencies and incentives of pluralism had won out over central direction; that decentralisation had triumphed over dirigisme.[43]

Governments tend to be centralist in their instincts. In practice, this has meant that market forces are rarely allowed to play a significant role in organising the production and distribution of those goods and services that governments supply. Government agencies also operate in a non-competitive environment, which discourages self-evaluation.[44] Since governments in the developed countries now spend on average about 37 per cent of national income,[45] these are significant deficiencies. One result is that public services, such as health, education and housing seem perpetually to be in crisis. Another is that large sums of consumers' and taxpayers' money are spent on perverse subsidies to sectors such as agriculture, road transport and energy. Perverse subsidies are for the most part economically inefficient *and* environmentally destructive.[46] They also favour the large and global over the small and local. So, for instance, in the US about 88 per cent of support to the agriculture sector goes to the largest (in terms of gross sales) 25 per cent of the farmers.[47] Perverse subsidies are significant: those for agriculture in the developed countries alone amount to more than $300 billion annually.[48]

Crumbling public services and billions of dollars in perverse subsidies: are governments and government-backed organisations like the United Nations any more efficient in allocating conflict-reduction resources? Unfortunately all these bodies' decisions about conflict reduction are subject to the same deficiencies as those of their contributing governments. They are centralised, unexposed to competition and, in almost all most cases, not subject to the disciplines of effective self-evaluation. Most of the time governmental conflict-reduction activities are also uncoordinated with those of non-governmental organisations (NGOs), whose own spending is probably more flexible and efficient.

Take as one example, the appalling Rwandan genocide, which highlighted the dependence of this centralised decision-making on the whims of the UN membership. In 1994 the UN was begging for troops to send to Rwanda after the genocide started, but the African states refused. By the time troops finally did go in to Rwanda, much of the genocide had already taken place.

Former officers of the now defunct private military company, Executive Outcomes, provided documentation showing how they could have had troops on the ground in Rwanda within two weeks of being called. 'For $150 million they could have ended the genocide—imagine how many hundreds of thousands of innocent African lives could have been saved. There is no imaginable way that the UN could do such a task so quickly and so cheaply.'[49] That is merely one, tragic, example of how the effectiveness of the UN was held back by the politics and infighting of its members. Anecdotal evidence of this kind does not prove that market forces are always superior to public sector approaches. But it does suggest that those charged with conflict-reduction should be able to use markets when doing so would be more efficient.[50] In that way, the efficiencies and incentives of the market could be injected into the achievement of the social goal of conflict reduction.

After all, these incentives operate all too freely in the market for the weaponry that creates so much mayhem and misery. So much so that world military expenditure in 2001 was estimated at $839 billion, accounting for 2.6 % of world gross domestic product and a world average of $137 per capita.[51] Global spending on arm procurement accounts for between 20-30 per cent of military spending, the bulk of which goes to operations, maintenance and personnel.[52] By contrast, extraordinarily few global resources are committed to the prevention, management, or resolution of the world's most prevalent wars, almost all of which take place in poor countries. Nor, in relative terms, is much spent on peacekeeping and post-conflict reconstruction. The annual budget for UN peacekeeping was about $2.60 billion in 2002 and is estimated at about $2.63 billion for the year to 30 June 2003.[53] Preventive diplomacy missions cost only a tiny fraction of this amount.[54]

Of interest too is that many of the late 1990s' most serious wars involved conflicts over the control of black market commodities and assets that can be easily liquidated through illicit trade, such as drugs and diamonds. In contrast to conflict-reduction, the global arms trade has become increasingly privatised,[55] and so is most probably realising the benefits that come from pluralism, in sad contrast to conflict-reduction agencies.

Voices calling for the introduction of the market's incentives and efficiencies in the field of conflict-reduction are muted. It is, though, worth noting that the US Libertarian Party has stated that if the US were threatened by an aggressor a

Libertarian President would warn the dictator that any aggressive act would prompt the posting of a mega-reward for the death of the dictator—a reward payable to anyone anywhere, including the dictator's guards and wives.[56]

Sadly, this market-and-outcome orientated approach was adopted by Saddam Hussein, the Iraqi dictator whose regime was brought to an end in April 2003. Until then he made payments of $25 000 to every family of Palestinian suicide bombers during the Israeli-Palestinian clashes that began in September 2000. Doing so he demonstrated an awareness of the value of economic incentives and specified outcomes, matched only by his loathsome intent. The US learned the lesson, perhaps too late: it subsequently offered millions of dollars to those who supplied information leading to the capture of the Saddam regime's chiefs.

The manifold complexity of conflicts, the proliferation of possible root causes, the intricacies involved in conflict-reduction: virtually all aspects of conflict cry out for a pluralist solution. The challenge is to find a way of subordinating these tendencies to the desired outcome of a lower level of violent political conflict. Recent years have seen some governments experiment with 'more market' approaches to the supply of some goods and services. Does their experience offer any guidelines for conflict reduction?

## *PRIVATISATION*

Privatisation is the selling of assets owned by government suppliers of services and the transfer of control to shareholders. Some governments have tried, often against entrenched opposition, to privatise certain services previously done by national or local government employees. In many countries utilities, such as railways, electricity companies and telecoms have been fully privatised. In the United Kingdom most of the local authorities' housing stock has been sold to ex-tenants. In some countries whole industries have been privatised. How successful have they been, and are there any implications for conflict reduction?

In those countries with rule of law and secure property rights it has had some success, at least when compared to the performance of nationalised industries. There have been some improvements in efficiency, and because of the taxes they pay on their profits, privatised companies now make positive contributions to government funds—a dramatic change from when they were publicly owned and were mostly a drain on public funds. But some of the labour the industries shed on privatisation has not found alternative employment, and it appears that it was government's disengagement from day-to-day operating decisions, rather than the transfer of ownership, that secured privatisation's efficiency gains.[57] Customers have on balance gained from privatisation, but not hugely. There have been significant improvements in service to customers where businesses have faced competition, as in telecoms and airlines. Fears that privatisation would lead to a loss of universal service or to higher charges for the poor have proved unfounded,[58] but again, regulatory policy has probably been an important factor. Privatisation, according to another view, has apparently created a need for very detailed public regulation of privatised industries, and this has been quite at odds with what was expected by the government and its advisors. What we have now 'is not a clear case of the state withdrawing as an economic agent but rather changing its role as such.'[59]

Under the right circumstances it does seem, however, that privatisation can be helpful as one way of giving more meaningful incentives for people to run certain services that used to be run by government agents.

Could conflict-reduction be privatised? This would take the form of a government, or several governments in a region, agreeing to sell their defence agencies to the private sector, which would then supply defence services. The problem insofar as conflict-reduction is concerned is that privatisation cannot work for public goods. These are goods that are:

- non-excludable: they cannot be confined to those who have paid for it. In this sense, non-payers can take a free ride and enjoy the benefits of consumption; and

- non-rival in consumption—consumption by one person does not reduce the availability of a good to others.

Conflict-reduction would be an archetypal public good, in that it would be supplied either to all members of a society or none. Other examples of public goods include flood control systems, street lighting and national defence. Public goods are not normally provided by an economy's private sector. Private companies have private goals. Their incentives are to maximise their revenues, given control of assets that currently lie with the public sector. They cannot do this if the goods or services are of a public nature. Citizens would want to become 'free riders', and would be able to do so for goods and services that are non-excludable. Free-riders could simply benefit from the provision of the good without paying for it. Privatisation is merely a transfer of assets, or a disengagement of government from the running of certain activities. By itself, it cannot supplant the government's role as a provider of public goods.

So national defence, and other public goods and services are provided collectively by the government, and then financed through taxation of individual households and businesses. This solution appears to have worked well enough for those fortunate to live in the industrialised countries over the past decades: it has certainly provided them with an effective deterrent to invasion from other countries. But it has not halted the threats from terrorism nor the proliferation of weapons of mass destruction. Nor can it be shown to be especially cost-effective. And it has certainly not brought about peace for countless millions who live in many developing countries. The countries' own governments are too poor, too powerless, too indifferent or too callous to provide their citizens with effective defences. The UN, NGOs and most governments in the industrialised world do have programmes aimed at reducing conflict in and between developing countries. But the efforts of those charged with such conflict-reduction are often undermined by the governments of the countries concerned who, rather than supply the public good of peace for their citizens, are often to be seen supplying the 'public bad' of conflict either internally or with other countries. Those—the vast majority—who would like to escape the consequences of such a policy can do little in the way of opting out of violent political conflict. And while we cannot say that conflict-reduction resources are deployed inefficiently, neither can we be sure that they are efficient. What is certain is that they have not been translated into near-universal freedom from actual or potential violent political conflict.

Privatisation of conflict-reduction activities, if it were feasible, would benefit at least the wealthier residents of these countries, who would then be able to purchase freedom from conflict. But the public good characteristics of peace—its non-excludability and non-rival nature—mean that even these people are denied the opportunity to live in peace. Private sector suppliers of political conflict-reduction services have not proliferated and one reason must be that under the current regime, they would not make an economic profit. Peace 'consumers' can take a free ride without having to pay for conflict-reduction services.

## CONTRACTING OUT

'Contracting out' means that government specifies the outputs it requires, in terms of the nature and level of service required, and invites the private sector to bid for the contract to supply these outputs. Some central and local government bodies that used to supplied goods or services in the past, now contract out certain of these functions to private sector bodies. In some US states, allocation of welfare benefits has been so contracted out; while in the UK, local authorities have put out to tender such services as hospital laundries, previously the province of the public sector.

Contracting out of services has been used as an efficient way of supplying carefully specified outputs. Specification of these outputs, as with regulating privatised utilities, can be a costly exercise (though costs will fall as different public sector bodies share their output-specification experiences), as is the monitoring of compliance, but allowing the private sector to bid to supply outputs is generally more efficient than paying directly from public funds. Could the UN or governments contract out conflict-reduction services to private bodies? To some extent they already do: the UN, for example, increasingly contracts out many of peacekeeping tasks. But because of the degree to which conflict-reduction outputs must be specified to ensure efficiency, contracting out of services generally tends:

- to be limited to particular stages of an outcome-delivering enterprise; and

- to reinforce established ways of doing things.

These features tend to limit contracting out to a narrow range of outputs, and to be short term in nature. Bidding for contracts would effectively be restricted to a limited number of established players, who would tend to do things in established ways.

What about making contracts to supply outputs tradable?

Standardised tradable contracts to supply specific goods at some future date ('futures') are very widely used in agriculture, and attract a great deal of participation. So too do markets for derivatives of shares, currencies, and share indices. Tradable output contracts would help enlarge the number of possible bidders for contracts, and so introduce more competition into the bidding process: bidders would know that their obligation to supply outputs would not be total. After carrying out some of the necessary output-delivery services, they could sell their contract, presumably for a price higher than the price they paid for it, to others who would continue the output-delivery service. Expanding the pool of possible bidders helps avoid the problem of collusion (tacit or not) between bidders for contract. In a small pool there is a greater likelihood that bidders will agree (explicitly or not) to inflate their bids.

Tradability of contracts would also encourage suppliers of services to continue to minimise costs and maintain efficiency *after* they have started helping achieve the targeted goal. Holders of non-tradable contracts or their employees have little incentive to maximise the speed and efficiency with which they go about supplying the agreed output. While contractors can sometimes benefit from being efficient, they cannot always enjoy this benefit in terms of immediate cash capital gains, and salaried employees very often have implicit incentives to be inefficient. There is scope for incentive payments, or penalty clauses, but these are crude, ad hoc arrangements that are costly to administer or impose.

Tradability would also transfer the risk of breach of contract from the tax-or rate-payer to bondholders. If, under a contract system, the successful bidders fail to do what they were legally obliged to do, then it is up to the aggrieved party—the central or local government agency—to take proceedings against them. Even if such actions are successful, they can be protracted and costly. Under a tradable contract regime, underperforming investors would find a ready market for their contract in people who believe they can be more efficient.

Tradable contracts, then, would appear to be an efficient way by with government bodies could open up the delivery of social outputs, such as conflict-reduction services, to the private sector. But there remains a fundamental problem: outputs are not outcomes.

## *OUTPUTS AND OUTCOMES*

Outputs, however efficiently supplied, do not necessarily lead to more favourable, or more efficiently supplied, outcomes and it is outcomes that matter to those affected by conflict (see box). So, for example, peacekeeping services are routinely contracted out, but those holding contracts are for the most part rewarded regardless of whether their efforts are successful or not at keeping the peace.

Even if market forces were introduced into the supply of conflict-reduction outputs, there would be a major problem: outputs do not necessarily bring about better outcomes.

---

### Essential terms

**Inputs** Resources used for reducing conflict, such as expenditure on conflict prevention; or spending on peacekeeping.

**Outputs** Products or services that are directly attributable to the performance of a conflict-reduction agency. Examples include: the number of patrols carried out by peacekeeping forces; firepower of weapons withdrawn from conflict areas by a decommissioning agency; proportion of time that communications and Information Technology services to a conflict-reduction agency are up and running.

*Outcomes* Desirable sets of circumstances, which are likely to be influenced by both an agent's outputs, and by factors outside agents' control. Targeted conflict-reduction outcomes could include: numbers of people killed by violent political conflict; numbers of refugees from conflict—see discussion in text below. The terms 'objectives' and 'goals' are used synonymously in this text to mean desired outcomes.

*Indicators* Quantifiable measures that can be used singly or in combination to chart progress towards objectives. Ideally these would be actual outcomes, or inextricably and closely correlated with outcomes. Good indicators of conflict therefore would be numbers of people killed directly or indirectly by conflict, or number of hours of martial propaganda emitted by a country's state-run broadcasting systems.

Could delivery of outcomes, as against outputs, be contracted out? And could it be done for conflict-reduction?

Governments, as we saw above, have tried to introduce more-market methods into achievement of some of their objectives. But they have been less willing to experiment with the stipulation of outcomes, as against outputs or other simplistic numerical targets.

In this respect it is worth looking at the experiences of the New Zealand public sector reforms, undertaken over several years beginning in 1988. In this short time, the New Zealand public sector was radically and innovatively reformed. Tightly held central control gave way to autonomous departments, headed by chief executives with the authority to take decisions relating to the whole of their organisations. Chief executives are now expected to hire and fire staff, negotiate pay, manage their finances and capital assets, negotiate purchase agreements and be held to account for outputs. Other relevant features of the New Zealand public sector are that:

- accountability for resources and results is maintained through contestable, contract-like arrangements within government;

- performance agreements between government ministers and chief executives lay down standards and expectations for department heads; and

- purchase agreements between ministers and departments specify the outputs to be produced during the year.

The arrangements between ministers and departments specify *ex ante* the outputs they are required to deliver, but leave chief executives free to select the mix of inputs to be used in producing these outputs. While innovative both in New Zealand and in comparison to other developed countries' reforms, the reforms were constrained by the then existing institutional structures. At the outset of the reform programme, government departments had been envisaged as achieving specific outcomes. But that vision did not carry through. Instead, outputs became the measure by which departments' performance is judged; the rationale being that the supply of outputs can be directly attributed to departments' performance, while outcomes can be influenced by factors beyond their control. As one commentator put it: 'outcomes are externalities in two-party relationships; therefore it is exceedingly difficult to assign responsibility for them.'[60] The need to assign responsibility arises only because the players—those charged with doing things—are largely known in advance. They are the existing government departments, of course. It would appear then that, in effect, the New Zealand reforms have subordinated results to what appears to be the overriding need to assign responsibility, which in turn, seems to be driven by existing institutional structures and relationships.

More recently, administrations in both New Zealand and the United States have looked in more detail at social outcomes. They have recognised that if they are to measure the effectiveness of policy programmes then outcomes have to be the focus rather than departmental outputs. As the US authorities put it 'The Results Act[61] [the relevant legislation] seeks to improve the management of federal programs by shifting the focus of decision making from staffing and activity levels to the results of federal programs.'[62] The Results Act seeks to improve the management of federal programmes by shifting the focus of decision-making from staffing and activity levels to results. Executive agencies are required to prepare five-year strategic plans to set general directions and then prepare annual performance plans that establish the connections between the long-term strategy goals and the day-to-day activities of the program managers and staff. Finally, the Act requires that each agency report annually on the extent to which it is meeting its annual performance goals and the actions needed to achieve or modify those goals that have not been met. All the relevant agencies have been challenged by the need to collect outcome data on an ongoing basis. These challenges included:

the time and the expense involved, grantees' concerns about their reporting burden, and substantial variation in states' data collection abilities.[63]

In New Zealand, the State Services Commission has looked at the evaluation of policy outcomes in the context of improving the quality of policy advice.[64] More recent New Zealand research has tried to refine the meaning given to outcomes.[65] The New Zealand Ministry of Social Policy has been working on the conceptual foundations of cross-sectoral social policy and social development.[66] The major problem, according to one commentator, appears to be one of devising appropriate indicators and setting up a suitable monitoring framework.[67] The time involved and the intellectual difficulty in generating such indicators make for slow progress; this issue, it is recommended, should be addressed at the policy development stage.[68]

The relevance of these experiences for our purposes is twofold:

First, there is an increasing recognition that the effectiveness of government policies can be best measured by focusing on outcomes, rather than inputs or outputs. And second, the monitoring of policy initiatives can generate new information needs, and that these are best addressed when the policies are being devised.

Note that this thinking from New Zealand and US is concerned with outcomes mainly for monitoring and evaluation purposes. There is no suggestion that institutions charged with achieving social outcomes be paid according to how successful they are in actually achieving them; or rather, since, outcomes are not fully dependent on departmental performance, according to how closely actual outcomes match up with desired outcomes. This leaves the risks of such an underachievement, whether caused by departmental underperformance or by external events, entirely in the hands of the funding body—generally a government agency, and so, ultimately, the taxpayer.

.So again, the new thinking appears to take the institutional structures as given. And it seems only just and natural that bodies should not be penalised if the outcomes they are charged with achieving are not reached because of circumstances that are beyond their control. Of course, such a system gives these bodies no incentive to look at these circumstances to try to bring them within their control, nor to manage the risks and so maximise their performance against those circumstances that cannot be controlled.

Providing incentive payments strictly correlated with performance against outcomes would help: but would be difficult to implement as agency staff, who would still be public sector employees, would again be effectively penalised if adverse circumstances made achievement of their target outcomes unachievable.

Making contracts to achieve social outcomes tradable would go some way toward solving that problem. The identity of those doing charged with achieving social outcomes would then be neither known in advance nor fixed. Such contracts to achieve social goals could be bought and held by anybody, not just agents directly involved in achieving the specified outcomes. And they could be traded at any time until the contract had been fulfilled. Tradable contracts would mean that the range of possible bidders would not be limited to a few likely operators, but would be open to all who are prepared to do, or to finance the doing of, projects that would help achieve the targeted objective. Competitive bidding for the contracts would discourage people from making excessive bids, so ensuring that social objectives would be achieved as cost-effectively as possible.

One problem is that tradable contracts to achieve major objectives, such as, for instance, peace in the Middle East, would necessarily involve very large investments, which would exclude from the bidding large numbers of possible contributors to such an outcome. Potential bidders for the contract would have to take on all the responsibility for furthering progress toward the specified outcome at any one time. Of course, once they had furthered such progress, they could then sell the contract to other bidders, who would advance progress further. And they could, of course, subcontract some, or all, of the projects they deem necessary to achieve the targeted outcome. But because of the need to take overall responsibility for the contract, it could be expected that the value of the contract would be so high as to exclude most bidders.

It is probably not for this reason that tradable contracts to achieve specified outcomes are rarely, if ever, used. More important obstacles are the practical difficulties of overcoming the mindset of government agencies, which would resist the handing over of responsibility for supplying domestic social and environmental services to the private sector. But perhaps, with a little tweaking, tradable contracts to achieve a specified outcome could be made more practical for large-scale conflict-reduction objectives. After all, there is still a lot to achieve in that area and, in contrast to the situation for social outcomes within countries, there is likely to be less opposition from vested interests currently engaged in trying to reduce conflict. Conflict Reduction Bonds, to be described in the next chapter, may be the answer.

# SUMMARY

The previous chapter argued that there are no easily identifiable root causes of war of practical value, such that their removal would inextricably remove the causes of armed political conflict. This makes peace building especially challenging. Compounding this difficulty is the complexity of conflict reduction itself. Consider some of the multitude of operations that can be included in a broad definition of conflict reduction: conflict assessment, conflict mediation, peace-keeping, arms verification, reconciliation, and re-integration of combatants. Most of these activities are currently performed by inter-governmental agencies, such as the United Nations, government agencies, academic bodies, non-governmental organisations or independent research institutes. In some cases their efforts to reduce conflict are by-products of programmes focused on other social problems. But more importantly, such resources as are devoted specifically to conflict-reduction are directed at activities or institutions, rather than any targeted outcome. And, unfortunately, the most important of these bodies are organised along the same lines as the governmental bodies in the developed countries that are charged with social and environmental responsibilities. They are centrally run, either by governments, or by intergovernmental agencies, and they do not explicitly reward the reduction of conflict but, like governments the world over, they subordinate the achievement of outcomes to current institutional structures and payment mechanisms.

The many non-governmental organisations, working diligently in conflict-reduction and related areas, suffer from similar problems. They are small, and while their own resources might be very well managed, and allocated in ways that maximise returns, they do not receive funds in proportion to their success or otherwise in their chosen field of endeavour.

What is needed then is a way of preventing or defusing war that is flexible enough to identify and deal with root causes when doing so will be the most practical and efficient way of reducing conflict, but that can also operate even when the causes or aggravating factors are obscure or intractable. No single solution is going to work. The world's conflicts arise from a multiplicity of causes. For some conflicts there might be nothing wrong with current methods: all that is needed are more resources. But for other conflicts, totally new solutions might be necessary, and people must be motivated to look for, find and use them. We cannot prejudge whether this conflict or that can best be solved by any particular method. Circumstances are always changing, and no conflict is exactly like any other.

An ideal solution then would encourage a range of diverse and responsive solutions. It would mobilise the interests of the large majority of people in every country of the world who want peace. It would find ways of co-opting or subsidising those people in positions of authority and power who want to build peace, and at the same time it would bypass, distract, or otherwise undermine, those opposed to that goal.

Ideally too, it would use market forces: the multiplicity of causes of armed political conflict, and the need for a wide range of diverse, adaptive solutions strongly suggest that market approach could be effective. If market forces could be harnessed into the achievement of a specific, targeted conflict-reduction goals, their pluralism and incentives would work better than current methods at directing scarce resources into their most efficient use. Greater efficiency in terms of conflict reduction per unit outlay could bring about double benefits: it would be an end in itself, but it could also attract more resources into conflict-reduction. Of the more-market approaches that can be used to generate diverse and responsive conflict-reduction solutions, tradable contracts to supply the desired outcome of peace appear to be most promising.

The rest of this paper describes a new financial instrument, Conflict Reduction Bonds, which are intended to channel the market's incentives and efficiencies into ending for all time what must surely be the world's most grievous social problem: war.

# 3

# *Conflict Reduction Bonds: an overview*

This chapter describes a new financial instrument, Conflict Reduction Bonds, designed to inject market incentives into the reduction of conflict.

## CONFLICT REDUCTION BONDS

Conflict Reduction Bonds would be issued by a trusted financial institution. They would be backed by governments, institutions or anyone else with a genuine interest in peace. These backers would make financial donations to a fund that would be used to redeem the bonds. If world peace were being targeted, most governments would, ideally, contribute to the redemption funds, perhaps in proportion to their Gross Domestic Product. If reductions in a regional conflict were targeted, governments in that region would probably be the largest backers.

Conflict Reduction Bonds would be issued on the open market and would become redeemable for a fixed sum *only when the targeted components of violent political conflict reached a very low level.* Importantly, the bonds would make no assumptions as to *how* to minimise conflict—that would be left to bondholders. They would specify peace outcomes, which can be simpler to measure and monitor, and more strictly correlated with society's wishes, than outputs. Partly for that reason they could be made more long term in nature.

Normal bonds are redeemable at a fixed date, for a fixed sum, and so yield a fixed rate of interest. Conflict Reduction Bonds would not bear interest and their redemption date would be uncertain. Bondholders would gain most by ensuring that the targeted reduction in conflict were achieved quickly. (Unless otherwise stated, hereafter 'bonds' refer to Conflict Reduction Bonds, rather than conventional bonds.)

Under the bond mechanism governments, with the help of the United Nations, NGOs and charities, would collectively decide on the exact specification of the targeted level of violent conflict, and contribute toward the funds needed to redeem the bonds. The bonds would be issued by open tender, as at an auction; those who bid the highest price for the limited number of bonds would be successful in buying them. Each bond would become redeemable for, say, $1 billion once the targeted level of peace, as certified by objective measurements made by independent bodies, had been achieved *and sustained*. Once issued, the bonds would be freely tradable.

Assume that Conflict Reduction Bonds, each redeemable for $1 billion, had been issued, and that they each sold for $100 million. People, or institutions, now hold an asset that gave them a return of 900 percent once the targeted peace level had been achieved. It is this prospect of capital gain that would give bondholders a powerful incentive to do what they can to end deadly conflicts, and to do so as cost-effectively as possible.

Once issued the bonds would be freely tradable on the open market. Governments—including those currently engaged in deadly conflicts—might decide to buy Conflict Reduction Bonds. So too might non-governmental militant organisations and others who are currently financing violence. Or the issuers might give the bonds to certain of these bodies as a form of aid. Ownership of Conflict Reduction Bonds would enable these bodies to reap financial rewards by ceasing to foment conflict. They could do this in ways they have not fully explored, because they have had no incentive to do so.

But Conflict Reduction Bonds, being tradable on the open market, could be bought by other institutions or individuals at any time until redemption. Whenever potential investors in the bonds thought they could reduce conflict more effectively than current bondholders, then they would be in a position to offer more than the current market value of the bonds to the existing bondholders, and buy them. The financial costs of failing to reach the required target would be borne by bondholders, rather than those contributing to the redemption funds.

Bondholders would have the means, motive and opportunity then to use their own capital, or borrow on the strength of the redemption value of their bondholdings, or on the strength of any increase in the value of their bonds, to support projects that would lower the level of violent conflict.

Note that the bond mechanism would be helped by the support and participation of governments or organisations actually engaged in conflict, but *it would not rely on such support*. The bonds might give rise to new, specialist organisations devoted to minimising violent political conflict as cost-effectively as possible.

These organisations could use their anticipated capital gains from bondholding to influence those people, whether or not they are active participants in conflict, who could do most to build peace.

What would determine the price of the bonds? Most obviously, the market's assessment of how close the peace target were to being achieved. Expected returns from other financial instruments will also be a factor. The bonds would sell for small fractions of their issue price if people thought there were virtually no chance of world peace being achieved in their lifetime. People would differ in their valuation of the bonds, and their views would change as events occurred that made achievement of the targeted peace objective a more or less remote prospect. But the bonds, once issued, would be transferable at any time. Bondholders, having contributed to a lessening of the conflict, would see the value of their bonds rise. They could then sell their bonds and realise a capital gain.

The market prices of Conflict Reduction Bonds would be publicly quoted, just like those of ordinary bonds or shares, and these prices, and their changes over time, would help those allocating conflict-reducing resources as effectively as possible-this feature is discussed at length in the next chapter.

## WHAT TO TARGET?

So crucial to Conflict Reduction Bonds' operation is the precise definition of the targeted peace objective, that it will be discussed both briefly here and in more detail in the annex to this chapter. It is not merely a technical issue. The incentives that the bonds put in place would encourage people to strive to achieve the components that make up the targeted objective, so it is important that these components coincide with society's interests.

The bonds could target an index comprising a wide range of indicators of conflict and peace simultaneously, over the entire world. An index could comprise various components including:

- Number of direct and indirect deaths resulting from armed conflict.
- Numbers of refugees fleeing armed conflict areas.
- Military spending, on both materiel and personnel.

These individual components could all be targeted simultaneously.

The bonds could be issued for different continents or regions, with different targeted definitions of peace to suit local conditions. For instance, bonds targeting peace in the Middle East could readily target numerical indicators of dead and injured, as these figures are well-documented in comparison to other conflicts. In regions where casualty numbers are unreliable other indicators would have to be targeted. These could include quality of life indicators, such as literacy, or the numbers of people moving across certain boundaries, or the value of weapons purchased by potential participants in conflict. Or conflict-related deaths could be estimated through demographic analyses of census data before and after conflicts, or through indirect mortality measurements such as survey questions on survival of siblings, parents, or spouses.[69] When appropriate, targets could be specified on the basis of random sampling of populations, with such components as 'proportion of interviewees who have lost one family member to violence' used, rather than unreliable aggregate casualty figures.

Conflict Reduction Bonds could also aim to achieve peace for specified periods: they could be redeemed once the targeted peace objective had been sustained for a period of five or ten years, say.

## PEACE AT ALL COSTS?

Before each issue of Conflict Reduction Bonds, the bonds' backers would have to decide approximately on the maximum they would be prepared to pay to see the targeted outcome achieved.

Depending on which governments are backing the bonds, and which area of (potential) conflict they are targeting, one consideration might be the financial benefit they might gain by reducing conflict. A significant reduction in a targeted conflict could allow the governments backing the bonds to divert spending away from the military and toward more edifying social or environmental services, or to lighten the tax burden on their populations. Added to this, though, would be the indirect benefits to participating governments (and others) who backed a Conflict Reduction Bond issue. Even if these governments did not envisage any reduction in their own military spending as a result of a reduced level of conflict, their economies could benefit financially from the greater political stability of their region. If, for example, some countries found it possible to reduce their military expenditure, their economies could grow, their imports would increase, and the rewards to bond backers in other countries could take the form of expanded exports.

Another source of benefit, seldom mentioned in the literature on military matters, but increasingly significant, would be the environmental gains from reduced conflict.

Of course, it goes without saying that peace is an objective in itself, independent of its economic or environmental benefits. The human cost of violent political conflict is worth reducing in its own right, though it resists quantification. Indeed, estimating any of the benefits from conflict-reduction is going to be problematic but, fortunately, those backing a Conflict Reduction Bond issue need not be overly precise in their calculations. They could start by issuing bonds redeemable for as much as they can reasonably afford to spend on reducing any particular conflict. From then on, much of the work necessary to quantify any reduction in conflict per dollar outlay would be done by bidders for Conflict Reduction Bonds on the open market.

To see this, assume again that bonds were to be used exclusively in pursuit of a 50 per cent reduction in some targeted measure of conflict, and that one thousand Conflict Reduction Bonds are issued, each redeemable for $1 billion once this measure had halved. If the market decided that the issue value of each of these bonds were $100 million, then the net cost to the backers of achieving the targeted objective (ignoring administration costs and inflation) would be $900 billion. In other words, the market at the time of issue believes that the cost, including its profit margin, of achieving the objective would be $900 billion.

But suppose the bond issuers are in the dark about how much it will cost to achieve a targeted objective and instead of issuing 1000 bonds they issue 10 000, each with the same redemption value of $1 billion. They would then be liable for a maximum cost of $10 000 billion ($10 trillion). However, the market would still reckon that it could achieve the targeted objective for around $900 billion. So instead of valuing the bonds at $100 million each, it would bid up the issue price of each bond to around $910 million. (Conflict Reduction Bonds would be an unusual financial instrument, in that the more that were issued, the higher would be their value!) The upshot of this is that the backers of the bonds would not have to estimate with any accuracy how much a targeted objective might cost to achieve, and they would put a cap on their total liability by limiting the number of bonds issued.

So the Conflict Reduction Bond mechanism would ensure that the market, rather than a handful of experts, decides roughly how much it would cost to reach a specified reduction in the level of violent political conflict. Participants in the market would do this when they bid for the bonds at issue and at all times afterwards. This fact, and the would-be bondholders' incentive to minimise their costs, contrast with the current system in which the costs of reducing conflict, if they are calculated at all, are not widely known nor subject to competitive bidding. Under the current system, in fact, many of the people charged with reducing conflict have subtle incentives to inflate the costs of their doing so. They will not do this maliciously, and might not even do so consciously, but it is probably fair to say that they are unlikely to be allocating their conflict-reduction resources with maximum efficiency simply because they have no incentive to do so.

Note that the issuing body could add to the number of Conflict Reduction Bonds in circulation after floating at any time if it wanted to boost the efforts going into the reduction of worldwide conflict. If it wanted, for whatever reason, to reduce such efforts, the situation would be a little more complicated. It could buy bonds back from holders, but doing so would reduce the total funds to be spent on achieving the targeted objective, and so would lower the value of all bonds in circulation. People might therefore be unwilling to buy bonds in the first place if they thought there were a high probability of the issuing body's buying some of them back in this way. They would demand some sort of premium for taking that risk. Alternatively, the issuing body could undertake either that it would never buy Conflict Reduction Bonds back or that, if it did, it would pay the market price ruling before it announced its purchase intentions.

What about the times when armed conflict is actually preferable to standing by and doing nothing? An ideal measure of conflict with worldwide application would aim to specify as targets for reduction not only the deaths resulting from armed political conflict between states but other problems, such as the persecution of minorities, to which well-intentioned, successful armed conflict is a solution. Importantly, the intention of most beneficial armed interventions is to prevent even worse, actual or threatened, violent conflict, so that, provided any target is sufficiently broad and long term, a bond regime need not discourage, and could actually encourage, effective preventive actions by well-intentioned armed force.

## WHAT COULD BONDHOLDERS DO?

Some people might buy Conflict Reduction Bonds as they would a lottery ticket, or a publicly quoted company share. They would think that their bonds' value might rise even if they did nothing to help achieve peace. Such passive investors would want to become 'free-riders' hoping to benefit from any increase in the bond price without actually participating in any peace-building activities. But the way markets work would limit the opportunities for this sort of investor. The more bonds these would-be free riders collectively owned, the more remote the targeted lower level of conflict would become, and so the more they would stand to lose as the aggregate value of their bond holdings fell. (A fuller discussion of free riding appears in chapter 5.) At some point, then, it would become worthwhile for these passive investors either to become, or to sell their bonds to, active investors.

Active investors would finance initiatives aimed at ending conflict. They could use their own capital, or borrow on the strength of the redemption value of their Conflict Reduction Bonds, or on the strength of any increase in the value of their bonds, to support projects that help reduce political violence. They would have every incentive to co-operate with each other to help achieve the targeted peace objective, and to do so as cost-effectively as possible. Their motivation would arise from the expected capital gain they would experience as the value of their bonds rose in line with the enhanced probability of the early reduction of targeted conflicts.

The lower the targeted level of political conflict the more likely bondholders would be to undertake projects that would pay off only in the long term. But it would be unsatisfactory to achieve a low level of violence just for a short period. The ultimate objective is a *sustained* low level of political violence, and that is how the targeted objective should be specified.

Bondholders could work to influence governments, including those of countries that supply the weapons that fuel conflicts. They could try to influence financial supporters of conflicts to redirect their funding into more edifying activities.

Bondholders could also lobby, or work with, governments to, say, give a higher priority to peace studies in schools, but they could also develop peace-teaching projects of their own. While immediate peace might not result, much more could be done to enhance the prospect of *peace in the future*. Bondholders could, for instance, make strenuous efforts in conflict-ridden regions to have some mixed classes of children of different nationalities, religion or ethnic origin at kindergarten and school. They could finance sports matches between opposing sides of current or potential conflicts. They could promote anti-war programmes on TV or set up exchange schemes for children or students of opposing sides. They might even subsidise intermarriage between members of different nationalities or religious communities. Simply by being non-governmental bondholders could be in a better position than governments to undertake peace-building initiatives of this sort.

Other examples of activities that bondholders could undertake would be:

- Lobbying for the elimination of all state-sponsored inflammatory propaganda, in textbooks, radio, TV, newspapers and the Internet.

- Lobbying western countries to improve trade access to poorer countries, so as to give developing countries the chance of economic growth.

- Promoting foreign direct investment into, conflict-ridden regions.

The rationale for the last two bullet points is to give the populations of these countries some means of becoming prosperous other than by plunder. Economic development would give people a chance to build trust and take a stake in a peaceful future and a better life for their children—a chance that many regimes still deny to their own people. More positively, it is to open the eyes of people to the virtues and rewards economic growth.

There are plenty of other activities that bondholders could back, including such mundane measures as promoting adherence to international treaties and laws, and improving data collection on violence. These are only examples, of course, though they do illustrate the potential for those in authority to undertake peace-building initiatives that they currently cannot, or do not want to, consider. In reality, bondholders would be likely to undertake a range of initiatives, *the precise nature of which need not be known in advance.* It would be up to bondholders to decide on those programmes that would give them the best return for each dollar they spend, and this means they would look for and put into action ways of achieving peace that they believe will be most effective.

Of course, some organisations do involve themselves in some of the activities mentioned above, but under a bond regime there would be a crucial difference: bondholders would have powerful incentives to ensure that the conflict-reduction projects they initiate or finance are as cost-effective as possible.

Much would depend on how long-term would be the targeted conflict-reduction objective. An ambitious conflict-reduction target would encourage bondholders to undertake indirect activities that have a long-term payoff. They could divert more funds into existing efforts at poverty reduction, improved governance and the strengthening of the rule of law. There is an emerging, though not unanimous consensus that democratic forms of governance are conducive to certain public goods including not only peace, but also human rights and economic development. In the words of a former UN Secretary-General, 'democracy contributes to preserving peace and security, securing justice and human rights, and promoting economic and social development.'[70] So bondholders might lobby governments to rule fairly and to represent all segments of their population in a reasonably equitable manner. Such efforts, already being made under UN auspices, could help diminish the appeal of extremist views that can lead to terrorism.[71]

Other activities could be undertaken in regions already torn by conflict, and that could erupt in violence again. These could include the disarmament, demobilisation and reintegration (DDR) of ex-combatants, considered crucial to achieving lasting peace after conflict.[72] Bondholders could encourage the inclusion of DDR programmes in peace agreements, and help finance rehabilitation and re-insertion packages for ex-combatants. They could forestall future conflict by helping ensure that all ex-combatants are treated equally regardless of former affiliations.[73]

## TRADING THE BONDS

Conflict Reduction Bonds, once floated, must be readily tradable at any time until redemption. The operation of such a 'secondary market' would be critical to the working of the bond mechanism. Many bond purchasers would want, or need, to sell their bonds before redemption, which might be a long time in the future. With a secondary market, these holders would be able to realise any capital appreciation experienced by their holdings of Conflict Reduction Bonds whenever they chose to do so. Tradability would make the bonds a more attractive investment in the first place.

As the bonds were traded, they would tend to flow towards those who would be most able to help reduce the targeted components of conflict. In fact, though, an actual flow of bonds would not be necessary. Large bondholders might simply decide to subcontract out the required work to many different agents, while they themselves would hold the bonds from issue to redemption. The important point is that the bond mechanism would ensure that the people who allocate the finance for conflict-reducing projects had an incentive to do so efficiently and to reward successful outcomes, rather than merely to pay people for undertaking activities. At the limit we can conceive of just one single buyer of all the bonds. If this buyer were determined to hold on to the bonds until redemption, then the bonds would function as a sort of performance-related contract, with the backers paying only when the objective had been achieved. The buyer could contract out most or all of the work required to achieve the objective, with the incentives given by the Conflict Reduction Bonds for speedy accomplishment cascading down from the bondholder to those subcontracted to do carry out conflict reduction.

Too large a number of small bondholders could probably do little to help achieve peace by themselves. If there were many small holders, it is likely that the value of their bonds would fall until there were aggregation of holdings by people or institutions large enough to initiate effective peace-building projects. As with shares in newly privatised companies the world over, Conflict Reduction Bonds would mainly end up in the hands of large holders—be they individuals or institutions. Between them, these large holders would probably acquire the majority of the bonds. Even these bodies might not be big enough, by themselves, to achieve much without the co-operation of each other. They might also resist initiating projects until they were assured that other holders would not be free riders. So there would be a powerful incentive for all bondholders to *co-operate with each other* to help bring about peace. They would share the same interest in seeing targeted objectives achieved quickly. So they would share information, trade bonds with each other and collaborate on conflict-quelling projects. They would also set up payment systems to ensure that people, bondholders or not, were mobilised to help build peace. Bondholders would either trade bonds or make incentive payments to ensure that any proceeds from higher bond prices, or from redemption, would be channelled in ways most likely to reduce conflict. Large bondholders, in co-operation with each other, would be able to set up such systems cost-effectively.

Regardless of who actually owned the bonds, aggregation of holdings, and the co-operation of large bondholders, would ensure that those who helped build peace were rewarded in ways that *maximise the reduction in conflict per unit outlay*.

## THE IMPORTANCE OF ECONOMIC INCENTIVES

Bondholders might not have to be terribly sophisticated in their choice of projects. Conflict Reduction Bonds would work on the principle that both bondholders and the people whom they pay (whether as agents or as recipients of, to put it bluntly, bribes) are motivated to some degree by financial incentives. Chapter 1 mentioned the conflicts in Lebanon, whose economic dimension has generally been underestimated. There are other cases, as complex as Lebanon, where economic incentives are not a root cause, but can prolong conflict. In Sierra Leone, following the Revolutionary United Front's insurgency, violence has been a means to pursue both political and economic ends. Rebel leaders, patrons abroad, opportunistic politicians, businessmen, Civil Defence Force commanders, peace-keepers, and even humanitarian workers have benefited from the war. Given the profit to be made during the war and the threat of retribution after the war, it is therefore not surprising that these various interests perpetuated conflict.[74] In conflicts such as these, bondholders might be able to reduce conflict quite directly and unsubtly simply by making appropriate financial transfers to certain individuals.

# CONFLICT REDUCTION BONDS AND TRADABLE CONTRACTS

How would Conflict Reduction Bonds compare with tradable contracts to deliver outcomes? The main difference is that the bonds would be more readily tradable than a single contract to achieve a measured quantity of conflict-reduction in a specific region. Bidders for the bonds could invest any sum they choose in the bonds (or shares of the bonds). They might not be able then individually to do much about achieving peace, but their bond holding could at least moderate their opposition to peace-building initiatives. And the bonds, or derivatives in the bonds, could serve as insurance for, say, companies that currently benefit from military spending.

Under a bond regime, bidding for the right to benefit financially from conflict-reduction would not be limited to a few likely operators, but would be open to all who are prepared to undertake, or to finance the undertaking of, projects that would help achieve the targeted objective. And it would be open *continuously*, from the time the bonds were issued until the time they were redeemed.

Compared with a single tradable contract to achieve a peace outcome, this continuous opportunity to buy and sell fractions of the contract would make ownership of Conflict Reduction Bonds more fluid. In turn, this would mean more market liquidity, more transparency and an enhanced ability for the government to fine-tune its priorities after the outcome has been specified and the bonds issued.

If the Conflict Reduction Bond concept were to generate more market activity, it would make more practical the targeting of remote objectives; ones that may take years or decades to achieve. Many businesses would be reluctant to take on such goals without the possibility that they could benefit in the shorter run. Conflict Reduction Bonds would allow them to do what they could to achieve the target, then benefit from selling their bonds at a higher price, letting the new bondholders continue the advance toward the goal.

Similarly, a liquid market for the bonds would make it more readily apparent that those charged with achieving a social goal had underestimated their costs, or overestimated their efficiency. With a single tradable contract, for which it would be unlikely there will be a liquid market, such deficiencies might take a fatally long time to become obvious. Of course, if a single agency purchased all the Conflict Reduction Bonds that were issued, the bonds would then function as a single tradable contract. And if this agency were determined to hold onto all the bonds until redemption, the bonds would operate as a contract to achieve the specified outcome, with a reward whose value to the supplier would increase with the efficiency and speed with which the peace objective is achieved. But under a Conflict Reduction Bond regime the market prices of the relevant bonds would fall, making it clear to everyone that the current contractors were inefficient, and making it easier for other investors to bid more for the bonds than they are worth to the current holders, and so take hold of the reins and pursue the targeted objective.

And, as we shall see in detail in the next chapter, there are other great advantages arising from the information generated by the bonds' market prices.

# ANNEX: WHAT SHOULD CONFLICT REDUCTION BONDS TARGET?

This annex looks in more detail at the desirable and feasible objectives of possible Conflict Reduction Bond regimes. Key criteria are that components of a targeted conflict-reduction objective should:

1. Represent, when targeted, ends in themselves, or be strongly and inextricably correlated to such ends, and

2. Be as easy as possible to measure objectively, reliably and accurately.

## *Possible elements for targeting*

Each conflict will have different characteristics, not least in how accurately measures of its effects can be quantified. Below are some possible starting points for compiling components to be targeted by a bond regime.

• Number of people killed in armed conflicts

Historically even the more basic questions about conflict, such as the identity of the combatants, when fighting began and ended and, more particularly, how many were killed, have been remarkably hard to pin down. Wars merged and split, or had no clear beginning or end.[75] Data on more recent conflicts, including internal conflicts, is still scanty, and different methodologies can produce different results. While armed forces and guerrillas usually know approximately how many people they have lost, they frequently understate the numbers killed on their own side, and overstate the numbers killed on the opposing side. Civilian casualties are even harder to pin down. In most conflicts there is no agency charged with counting them, and what figures can be found are clouded in uncertainty, imprecision and confusion. It is a general assumption that most casualties of war today are civilians, but estimates of the proportion vary considerably. It is harder to measure the numbers indirectly killed by conflict, through such consequences of conflict as flight, destruction of infrastructure or disruption of the economy. It is difficult to extract consistent and reliable quantitative information from the historical record.

- Expenditure on armaments

This has the advantage that it is strongly correlated with benefits forgone; that is, it represents the quantity of goods and services that could otherwise have benefited people. Thus, for example, the US and Soviet Union's very large expenditure on nuclear weapons and delivery systems during the Cold War did not translate into direct battle casualties. In the narrow terms of avoiding nuclear conflict, then, the Cold War can be said to have been successful.[76] But the expenditure on nuclear weaponry represents a large diversion of resources away from more valuable sectors of the countries' economies. Nor was it certain throughout the Cold War that conflict *would* be avoided, so there was a high price paid in personal anxiety and fear by large numbers of people in both countries and beyond. And while the former superpowers have reduced their nuclear weapons arsenals, they continue to hold a huge number of nuclear strategic offensive weapons, which could readily destroy Russian or American society. The decommissioning of nuclear material on both sides has generated environmental concerns.

It might also have accelerated proliferation. An ideal measure of conflict for a bond regime that targeted large-scale, or even worldwide, conflict levels should probably encompass not only expenditure on weapons, but also their distribution. India, Pakistan, Israel and North Korea can be regarded as already nuclear.

Iran is believed to be moving rapidly toward acquiring nuclear weapons, while Libya and Syria might also be moving in that direction.[77] The western world has been surprised in the past by the speed at which countries have developed nuclear weapons.[78] Even more frighteningly weapons of mass destruction are becoming available to private syndicates of all kinds that are not within the jurisdiction of the United Nations or any other body. The possibility of nuclear proliferation gaining further ground and jeopardizing regional and global stability is very real. And nuclear delivery systems, as well as chemical and biological weapons have also proliferated.

So there is a strong case for including, as components of a bond issue aimed at reducing worldwide conflict, both spending on weaponry in general and some quantifiable measure of proliferation of weapons of mass destruction in particular.

If a range of conflicts is being targeted by a single bond issue, national expenditures could be weighted on a Purchasing Power Parity basis, to approximate the true value of the benefits forgone, and the greater threat posed by similar dollar expenditures on weapons in areas where they cost less. For example, the same sum spent on smalls arms in African conflict areas could be weighted more heavily than if it were spent on routine maintenance of sophisticated western defence systems. Unfortunately, some components of military expenditures are often treated as state secrets. As well, defence industry structures are very often highly concentrated, or nationalized, making it difficult to obtain data or even good price estimates for military equipment.[79]Nor is there a complete authoritative record of global military expenditure.[80] But for particular conflicts, or potential conflicts, military spending could be one useful component of a conflict-reduction objective

• Military strength

Military strength is an estimate of both military personnel and military equipment. The rationale for including this measure is similar to that for including military expenditure: it represents both the opportunity cost of resources lost to the life-enhancing parts of the world economy, and it is an indicator also of the potential for violence, and so an indicator of human insecurity or anxiety. While estimates of materiel could be subject to the same imprecision as spending on armaments, numbers of military personnel might be easier to quantify for targeting purposes in some regions of actual or potential conflict.

• Mass media indicators of impending conflict

Conflict Reduction Bonds could also target events that are likely to lead to war, such as efforts to gain public support. There appears to be strong evidence that the underlying intentions of governments can be accurately gauged by a systematic analysis of opinion-leading articles in the mass media, regardless of the relative openness of the media in question. Such analysis allows the prediction of both the likelihood of conflict and what form of conflict—military, diplomatic or economic—will occur.[81] This sort of indicator could be useful as a target where military conflict has not begun, but appears possible, and where other data are scarce.

## *Discussion*

Whether these, or other, indicators are made the explicit target of Conflict Reduction Bonds depends on the intentions of the bonds' backers.

Take the Cold War, during which the US and Soviet Union spent vast sums on their nuclear weaponry, none of which was actually deployed. Should Conflict Reduction Bonds aim to reduce such spending? Or should we take the view that, since direct armed conflict between the two protagonists did not actually occur, then the sums spent on nuclear weapons would not have made sensible targets for a bond regime launched in the Cold War's early years? There are sound arguments on both sides. Certainly, the expenditure represented not only direct non-military benefits forgone by both economies (and indirect benefits, arising from lower exports, for example, forgone by other economies), but the *potential* for devastating conflict. For both reasons, it would make sense to allocate it some weight as an indicator in a bond issue addressing a broad, worldwide definition of conflict. On the other hand, where less devastating military conflict is actually occurring, or is a strong possibility, it might make more sense to attach more weight to such targets as battle or civilian casualties, rather than an expenditure indicator that might anyway be more difficult to calculate accurately.

One danger to be borne in mind when selecting targets, or combinations of targets, for a bond issue, is the possibility that a bond issue targeting one component of a particular conflict might encourage behaviour that aggravates other, untargeted, conflicts or components of conflict. A bond regime focussing on region A, for example, divert conflict-reduction resources away from region B. Or focusing on, say, numbers of armed personnel could encourage a government or military faction to switch spending away from recruitment and into arms purchases. As an ideal, objectives that if not pursued jointly could conflict, should be targeted by a single bond issue. But in most circumstances this would not be necessary, particularly in relation to actual or potential conflicts in which weapons of mass destruction are not an issue. It is quite likely, for example, that if numbers of personnel were reduced, then arms purchases would reduce too, or the capacity of existing materiel to inflict casualties would fall in parallel. As well, provided a bond regime targeted such obvious and meaningful outcomes as reduced numbers of people killed in conflict, it is unlikely that leaving out other indicators like military expenditure would actually cause these indicators to move in a negative direction. These indicators, in general, are correlated sufficiently strongly with the obvious targets to be safely left untargeted. The same can probably be said of the effects of conflict on a region's physical or social infrastructure, or the damage done to the physical environment.

What about United Nations missions, or other undertakings that involve the use of arms for, supposedly, peacekeeping purposes, or for pre-empting larger conflicts? Should the casualties of such 'beneficial' military interventions be included in total casualties to be targeted by a bond regime? Since the aim of these military missions is generally to reduce actual or potential military conflict, then it would be consistent to include the results of casualties they cause in any bond issue that encompasses the region within which they occur: the bonds would then encourage 'beneficial' military interventions insofar as they were successful in reducing the total number of long-term casualties in the region.

As a long-term ideal, a single issue of Conflict Reduction Bonds could target the effects of conflict worldwide, with each negative effect being weighted according to its lethality. Such a bond issue would encourage optimal allocation of the world's conflict-reduction resources. It would thus be theoretically superior but perhaps less feasible, to bond issues with more localised objectives. But in fact, people are already making efforts to calibrate warfare events and their impacts on societies, and these efforts could form the basis of a future target for bonds.

One example is the ten-point scale used by the Center for Systemic Peace.[82] The numbers on this scale represent a categorical indicator of the destructive impact of each violent episode on the directly-affected society, similar to that used to gauge the destructive potential of storms and earthquakes. The scale ranges from 1 (low damage and limited scope) to 10 (total destruction). On this scale, the Rwandan genocide of 1994 rates a 7, the ethnic war in Kosovo is rated 4, and the US and UK air campaign against Iraq in 1998-1999 rates a 1. Magnitude scores reflect the widest range of warfare's consequences to both short-term and long-term societal well-being, including direct and indirect deaths and injuries; sexual and economic predation; population dislocations; damage to cooperative social enterprises and networks; diminished environ-mental quality, general health, and quality of life; destruction of capital infrastructure; diversion of scarce resources; and loss of capacity, confidence, and future potential. The magnitude scores are considered to be consistently assigned across episodes and types of warfare and for all societies directly affected by the violence. For this reason it could form the basis of a worldwide Conflict Reduction Bond issue, as it would encourage the impartial allocation of society's scarce conflict-reduction resources into whichever conflict-reducing activity would do the most good, anywhere in the world, and regardless of the preoccupations of politicians, the public, or the media.

Work is also being carried out into a Human Insecurity Index, based on indicators such as the number of deaths from armed conflict, the incidence of criminal violence and refugee numbers.[83]

More realistically, in the short and medium term and for most conflicts, it would be reasonable to assume that the effects of conflict calibrated by all-embracing indicators of this type are sufficiently correlated with such more readily measured quantifiable indicators as deaths resulting directly or indirectly from conflict. So while aggregate indices of worldwide conflict will be helpful, it is certainly not worth waiting for broad, rigorous measures to be defined and compiled before attempting to target more obvious targets as 'number of people killed in conflict'. As well, a bond regime need not operate in a vacuum. While it could target the number of people killed in a conflict, other measures could be in force at the same time as a bond regime. For example, there could be treaty obligations to limit the number and type of weapons deployed, or numbers of armed personnel. The bond concept, fortunately, is a versatile one, and could be adapted to changing circumstances, or evolving views about which elements of conflict are best suited for targeting.

All such elements should, for bond redemption purposes, be measured by accredited impartial bodies. It is likely that there will always be some subjectivity about even the more verifiable of targeted goals, such as the number of people directly killed by conflict. Accordingly, the body that verifies and promulgates the measurements of whichever goals are targeted will have to be impartial, trusted, and beyond reproach.

# 4

# *Advantages of Conflict Reduction Bonds*

Conflict Reduction Bonds would build a coalition of interests with a strong incentive to reduce deadly violence as effectively and efficiently as possible. Their main advantage over existing peace-building initiatives would be their efficiency, but this overlaps with other advantages, including transparency and stability of the policy objective.

## *EFFICIENCY*

Efficiency gains, expressed as the reduction in violent political conflict worldwide per dollar expended, would arise from several linked sources.

Self-interest and market forces would channel conflict-reducing resources into achieving the desired *outcome* efficiently. This contrasts with the current system under which funding is generally allocated to organisations that may be well-meaning, but that are not rewarded in ways that correlate with their success in reducing conflict. A coalition of bondholders would have more freedom to initiate projects that governments and others in positions of power cannot support, or do not wish to support, or *do not wish to be seen* to support. Holders of Conflict Reduction Bonds would have incentives to support whichever conflict-reducing initiatives would be most effective. Their objective and that of the people who would back the bonds would therefore be *exactly the same*. The more efficient were bondholders in reducing the level of violence, the more they would gain from appreciation in the value of their bonds. This efficiency would maximise the reduction in violence that could be achieved per dollar outlay.

Of course, many enlightened individuals and organisations are already carrying out valuable peace-enhancing activities. But under a Conflict Reduction Bond regime many more might be enticed to do so, while very large numbers of people could be encouraged to moderate their opposition to measures that build peace. Importantly, under a bond regime, funds for building peace could bypass corrupt people in authority or inefficient governments or, by appealing to their financial self-interest (if they were bondholders, or bribed by bondholders) could effectively modify their behaviour in favour of achieving the targeted peace objective.

Many world conflicts occur within or between developing countries. Unfortunately, even more than in the rich countries, the stated objectives of politicians and governments differ from their real intentions. In many developing countries powerful politicians use their own hidden networks of placemen in key positions in important ministries to frustrate whatever projects or policies they find inconvenient. Outsiders, including especially overseas aid donors, find little correlation between what the governments in these countries say they want and what they actually want. World Bank and International Monetary Fund personnel officially judge countries on their stated policies and plans, but in many countries these bear little relationship to the way the country is actually run.[84] So it is important that ways of reducing conflict can circumvent any obstructions put in their path by such governments, and Conflict Reduction Bonds allow that possibility.

It would be in the interests of bondholders and those whom they influence to seek out those ways of achieving the targeted reduction of conflict that would give them the best return on their outlay. But this would also be in the interests of those, whether taxpayers or private individuals, who would be the ultimate source of funds used to redeem the bonds. Crucially, it would be only when the violence had fallen to the targeted lower level and been sustained for the stipulated period that the bond backers would end up paying for these efforts. Until then it would be up to bondholders to finance those initiatives that they believed would bring about reductions in the violence. Again, this contrasts with the current system, in which taxpayers incur costs for funding conflict-reduction schemes regardless of whether they are effective or not. The body that issues Conflict Reduction Bonds would, in effect, be contracting out the achievement of peace to the private sector. It would still, though, stipulate the definition of conflict that it wanted to see reduced and, by undertaking to redeem the bonds, would still be the ultimate source of finance for that reduction.

Bondholders could consider a wider range of possible activities than those bodies currently involved in conflict-reduction. Governments have real difficulties in investigating new approaches to social problems. The previous chapter mentioned some possibilities, such as subsidising intermarriage between fractious communities. As with many social programmes, government is subject to constraints on its behaviour that can limit its effectiveness. Actions such as subsidising intermarriage would arise intense ire, and could be explosively controversial, if undertaken by a national government or by an inter-governmental body such as the United Nations. It would be less controversial if undertaken by bondholders. Assume that bonds specifically targeting long-term peace in the Arab-Israeli conflict are issued. Then the only question bondholders need ask themselves about subsidising intermarriage between Palestinian Arabs and Israeli Jews is whether it would be cost-effective as a peace-building measure.

Governments' reluctance to explore new approaches to many social problems arises not only from the controversy that a particular new approach might generate, but also because government is generally more interested in preventing failure than in rewarding success. Government and inter-governmental organisations tend to believe that they should carry out only those activities that can plausibly be justified on the basis of a past record. These activities need not be very efficient, or even partly efficient. As far as government bodies are concerned they need only to have been tried in the past and not to have been publicly identified as disastrous. This is not a strategy designed to optimise performance; nor is it even designed to minimise failure. Rather it is designed to minimise the *public exposure* of failure. In the almost total absence of a self-evaluative culture[85] it leads to the continuing of inefficient, unimaginative activities. As the persistence of violent political conflict and other social and environmental problems shows, it is not a successful strategy.

Another source of efficiency arises from the greater freedom bondholders would have to ignore the priorities of the media. Conflict in the Middle East, for example, has a very high media profile; conflict in Africa, on the other hand, rarely makes the news. The 20-year long civil war in Sudan has led to the deaths of at least two million people, the displacement of millions more and a continuing (in mid 2003) serious humanitarian situation in the south of the country. The death toll in the five years since Congo's civil war began in 1998 is put at between 3.1 million and 4.7 million.[86] These wars rarely features in the western media. The result is that a disproportionate share of the world's meagre conflict-reducing resources flow to the Middle East, while the wars and civil wars of Africa, which have devastated the lives of millions, receive comparatively little attention. Holders of bonds aimed at minimising conflict over the entire world would allocate resources impartially, giving most attention to reducing those conflicts that, in their judgement, would maximise the conflict reduction that could be achieved per dollar outlay.

International bodies, and inter-governmental agencies share other unfortunate characteristics with national governments. They tend to adopt uniform approaches to similar problems, and they are slow to respond appropriately to rapidly changing circumstances. These deficiencies are apparently inherent in bureaucracies and result from there being no incentives to come up with more diverse or more adaptive solutions to social problems. They have probably contributed to the persistence of social problems in the rich countries, despite the ever-increasing expenditure allocated to their solution. And they can have the same effect internationally. Unlike government employees, however, holders of Conflict Reduction Bonds would have incentives to react to different conflicts in different ways, and to respond quickly and appropriately to events. They would also have incentives to monitor, improve and evaluate these diverse responses and they would have powerful incentives to discard the least promising of their approaches and to follow only those that had been successful and cost-effective in reducing conflict.

Under a Conflict Reduction Bond regime, if bondholders were unexpectedly efficient, or if external events were unexpectedly helpful, they could sell their bonds and realise their capital gains. But if bondholders were inefficient, or external events were unexpectedly unhelpful, so that bondholders failed to achieve the conflict-reduction target then *they* would be the losers, not the backers of the bonds. If the bonds were backed by various countries' governments, the ultimate beneficiaries of this feature of Conflict Reduction Bonds would be the taxpayers of contributing countries who, in a departure from the current system, would not have to pay for ineffective conflict-reduction projects.

## EFFICIENT COSTING

The resources that can be devoted to ending conflict are finite. They should therefore be channelled into those initiatives that can bring most benefit per unit outlay. In chapter 3 we saw how markets for Conflict Reduction Bonds would enable potential investors and others to gauge the effectiveness or otherwise of their conflict-reducing policies. This would make it unnecessary for bond backers to gauge precisely how much to spend on achieving a particular targeted reduction in conflict. Potential investors in the bonds would have estimated how much the targeted objective would cost to achieve, and would have every incentive to minimise this cost. They would do this when they bid for the bonds at issue *and at all times subsequently*, until the bonds were redeemed. At the same time, the bond issuers could put a cap on the backers' total liability by limiting the number of bonds issued.

These facts, and bondholders' incentives to minimise their costs, contrast with the current system in which the costs of containing conflicts, if they are estimated at all, are not widely known, nor subject to competitive bidding. A further point is that the issuers could add to the number of bonds in circulation after floating, at any time, if they wanted to boost the efforts going into peace-building initiatives.

But the bond mechanism would not merely minimise the total cost of achieving its specified objective. It would also indicate the *marginal* cost of achieving further reductions in the level of conflict. Assume that one million Conflict Reduction Bonds were issued targeting the reduction in some Conflict Index from 50 to 40 units, and that each bond becomes redeemable for $10 million once that objective has been achieved. Further, assume that each bond sells for $5 million each. This would tell the backers of the bonds that the present value of the expected *maximum* cost, including bondholders' profits, of reducing the Conflict Index from 50 to 40 units would equal $5 billion. Now assume that the bonds' backers decide to be more ambitious, and aim for a further fall in the Conflict Index to 30 units. It could issue an additional million Conflict Reduction Bonds, again redeemable for $10 million each, only when this new lower level of conflict were reached. These new bonds would (probably) each have an initial market value of less than $5 million, reflecting the (probably) diminishing returns involved in lowering the level of violent political conflict. But the main point is that, by letting the market do the pricing of the bonds, the bonds' backers would be getting an informed view of the marginal cost of their objectives. So if the bonds targeting the new Conflict Index level of 30 units were to sell for $4 million each, then the maximum cost of achieving that objective would be $11 billion, being equal to: $5 billion (paid out when the index fell from 50 to 40 units) plus $6 billion (paid out when the index fell from 40 to 30 units). The market would thus have revealed that marginal cost of a 10-unit drop in the Conflict Index had risen from $5 billion to $6 billion. Should the bond issuers aim for a further fall in the Conflict Index to 20 units? *After having issued Conflict Reduction Bonds and followed their progress, they would have robust information about the cost of doing so.*

This is, of course, a simplified example and in fact the bond market would continuously update its pricing information. Say that some new and promising conflict-reduction programme is announced. It could be technological, political or social—for our present purposes, the form it takes does not matter, but let us assume that it takes the form of an information-sharing agreement, and that this makes countries feel more secure.

How would the market for the same Conflict Reduction Bonds react to such a development? On the announcement of the new agreement the value of all the bonds would rise. Instead of being priced at $5 million and $4 million, the bonds described above might then sell for $8 million and $7 million. The total cost to the backers of redeeming these bonds would not change: it would remain at $11 billion (though redemption would most probably occur earlier). But the market would be generating new information as to the likely cost of future reductions in the level of conflict. The market would now be expecting reductions of 10 units of the Conflict Index to cost $2 billion (from 50 to 40 units), and $3 billion (from 40 to 30 units). The new information-sharing agreement would have reduced the costs from $5 billion and $6 billion, respectively. So the cost of any further conflict reductions would also fall, and by following the bonds' market price movements policymakers could gauge approximately by how much.

These figures are hypothetical, but they do indicate the role that markets for Conflict Reduction Bonds could play in helping the governments, international organisations and taxpayers who finance conflict-reduction decide on their spending priorities. The importance of this sort of market information can hardly be exaggerated. The failure in history of central planning can plausibly be attributed to the absence of market-generated information.[87] Market prices reflect all of the information used by all who transact, or choose not to transact, in the market. Central planning fails in comparison with a market economy because it encounters the limits of human beings' calculating capacity: no individual or group of individual planners knows or feasibly can know all the dispersed information that is embodied in prices. It limits the number of decision makers and so the ability to adapt to changing circumstances. Even with a sound incentive system in place—and the centrally planned economies had some fearsome systems—without the information that only markets can generate the computational task of organising an efficient allocation of resources is too great. Prices incorporate and simplify all of the dispersed information implicit in getting a product or service to the marketplace. Markets for Conflict Reduction Bonds would continuously generate and reveal this information to policymakers and all those involved in achieving social and environmental outcomes—probably for the first time on a systematic basis. A Conflict Reduction Bond regime would combine market information with incentives to use it efficiently: the synergies arising could be of enormous benefit to society as a whole.

We saw in chapter 3 that Conflict Reduction Bonds, compared with a tradable contract to reduce conflict, would enhance the backers' ability to adjust the resources they allocate to conflict-reduction after setting the objective. But Conflict Reduction Bonds have another advantage over a tradable contract to achieve peace. Such a contract could be traded, but it would be held by a single entity. This entity would decide whether or when the contract could be traded. Potential purchasers would have to buy the whole of the contract, and they would also have very little information as to how much it would be worth: there would be no market, with its multiplicity of participants, generating information as to the value of the contract. The size of the contract, and the lack of market information, would deter large numbers of potential participants in conflict-reduction from bidding for it. Conflict Reduction Bonds, on the other hand, would be continuously traded. The continuous availability of the market value of the bonds and their derivatives would encourage much greater participation than would a tradable contract held by a single agency. And the splitting of that contract into a number of bonds would lower the threshold at which interested parties could become actively involved as potential beneficiaries of a conflict-reduction campaign.

So, to recap, markets in the bonds would continuously reveal information that would tell the bonds' backers and anyone who might want to supply conflict-reduction services: (1) how close a targeted objective were to being achieved; (2) the potential rewards from buying the bonds and participating in objective-achieving projects; and (3) the likely costs of marginal improvements beyond those already targeted.

## *STABILITY*

A further advantage of Conflict Reduction Bonds would be the stability of their objectives. Many conflict-reduction programmes will have a necessarily long lead time, and bondholders should not be deterred from initiating them by fears of a change of policy. Under a bond regime only the ends of policy, not the means, would be specified. Current efforts to reduce conflict often depend on particular people or governments remaining in power. Or their success depends on how accurate are particular views about the causes of a conflict, or the nature of the protagonists. As events and circumstances change, these conflict-reduction efforts are often slow to adapt. But under a Conflict Reduction Bond regime bondholders would be free to choose what they believe will be the best ways of achieving peace as cost-effectively as possible. The goal of reduced conflict is more stable over time than the best ways of achieving it. So the bonds would lead to a rational allocation of conflict-reduction resources. Bondholders would maximise their returns by refusing to overestimate the importance of high-profile, short-term events. Motivated by profit, they would undertake activities that might bring peace only in the long term. These could include such unglamorous and slow-to-act projects as investment in education or in efforts made to end hate propaganda directed at children. There are people and organisations involved in these activities nowadays, but under a Conflict Reduction Bond regime it is likely that their efforts would receive more funding. Stability of the policy objective, reduced conflict, would give bondholders more confidence to invest for the long term.

## TRANSPARENCY

Another significant advantage of Conflict Reduction Bonds would be their *transparency*. The objectives of each bond issue would be clear and explicit. Their over-arching aim would be: to reduce the level of one or more violent political conflicts to a very low level. The bonds' redemption terms would thus make clear to everybody exactly what are the real objectives of those governments, NGOs, and individuals that back the bonds.

Some powerful people in governments, militant organisations or religious institutions would resent the targeting of such objectives by external agencies in this way. But, while under the current system they can oppose peace in ways that attract support, under a Conflict Reduction Bond regime, they would have to openly declare their opposition to peace itself. It is precisely this clear focus on the *outcome* of peace—rather than activities, policies, programmes or institutions—that would help mobilise and motivate the coalition working to achieve it.

By focusing on transparent outcomes, rather than activities, Conflict Reduction Bonds would encourage indirect, as well as direct, means of achieving them: efficiency in conflict-reduction would be the overriding criterion. This could bring about changes in the way organisations operate. An aid organisation, instead of focusing solely on, say, the number of households newly supplied with water, would also consider the potential of its activities to reduce conflict. Under a bond regime, it would divert resources into water-supplying initiatives that contributed more to conflict reduction and away from than those that in its view would do little or nothing to reduce conflict, or could even aggravate it.

Being transparent about their objective, Conflict Reduction Bonds would encourage constructive participation in the political processes leading to decisions on what exactly the bonds should target. At least as important, a government-backed bond regime would make explicit the maximum value that society wished to place on targeted cuts in levels of conflict. These would have to be openly decided and before any bonds could be issued. Costing outcomes in this way would make the tradeoffs between different conflict-reduction objectives, or between competing global concerns, more transparent.

## MORE ATTRACTIVE MONEY FLOWS

A further advantage of Conflict Reduction Bonds over conventional peace-building programmes is that, in many cases, they would have more politically appealing money flows. Current methods of conflict reduction can, for example, involve costly intervention by peacekeeping forces, for which taxpayers of contributing countries have to pay in advance of any actions, and regardless of these forces' success or otherwise. Conflict Reduction Bonds, however, would involve no advance payments by taxpayers. Bondholders would be rewarded only once they had successfully reduced conflict. The bonds would of course be redeemed by funds from the backing governments' general revenues, and taxes would still have to be levied to provide these but there is, nevertheless, a presentational advantage.

The other, more significant, money flow advantage of Conflict Reduction Bonds is that the participating governments would incur expenditure only when a reduction in conflict had been achieved and sustained. For this reason, the bonds may attract greater political support for certain causes than agency-or activity-based programmes.

## CORRELATION WITH PUBLIC BENEFIT

A less obvious benefit of a Conflict Reduction Bond regime would arise from the existence of a means of acquiring wealth whereby private gain would be strongly and inextricably correlated with social benefit. Many bondholders, whether institutions or individuals, would start out rich and, if their bonds rose in value, would become richer. But working successfully to achieve build peace would most likely be seen as a laudable way of acquiring wealth. There are intangible benefits from having people or institutions grow rich in this way. There are many disaffected people who, in some cases no doubt justifiably, view with suspicion or alarm the very high incomes or (apparent) profits of corporations engaged in activities of little obvious net social or environmental benefit. They are also unconvinced that 'trickle-down' occurs to any meaningful degree. Wealth, in these people's eyes, is the result of the abuse of human or environmental resources. Conflict Reduction Bonds could help alter this worldview.

# 5

## *Potential pitfalls*

Conflict Reduction Bonds would represent a radical change in the way in which our society does things. At first sight, a bond regime may even seem outlandish: it would appear to mean governments' handing over to the private sector their responsibility for achieving peace. It would also allow bondholders, whether they be governments of other countries, international bodies or private companies, to profit from the public purse. So it is important to realise that under a Conflict Reduction Bonds regime governments would merely be contracting out the *achievement* of conflict reduction. Governments, in agreement with each other and in consultation with their citizens, would still define the scope of bond issues, and they would specify the exact definitions of the conflict-reduction goals that they would pay to achieve. As backers of the bonds, it is they who would be undertaking to redeem the bonds and it is they who would still be the ultimate source of finance for the projects that achieve them. Moreover, competitive bidding for Conflict Reduction Bonds would bid away excessive private sector profits.

People would need to be reminded of these facts when asked to contemplate a bond regime. Nevertheless, the concept does present some possible pitfalls. Could free riders or derivatives markets undermine operation of a bond regime? Could a bond regime generate perverse financial incentives? This chapter looks these questions.

## THE FREE RIDER QUESTION

Some people or institutions might purchase Conflict Reduction Bonds with the idea of doing nothing but holding on to them until they could sell them at a profit. Such passive investors would have no intention of doing anything to help reduce conflict. Some of them could be casual purchasers who would buy bonds (or shares in a bond) with the same expectation as they would a lottery ticket.

They would hope to hold onto their investment until the bonds' market value had risen sufficiently high for them to enjoy a worthwhile capital gain. Other passive investors might be speculators who thought that the likelihood of the targeted objective being achieved quickly were greater than the rest of the market believed it to be—in other words, that the bonds were underpriced.

Another category of passive investor might be the hedger. These are people who, in the absence of the bond issue, would stand to lose if the conflict reduction target were achieved. They could be suppliers of weapons or other equipment to the military, fearful of losing contracts as a result of reduced political tension. Hedgers might buy the bonds as a form of insurance against that possibility.

Casual purchasers and speculators would want to become 'free riders', hoping to benefit from any increase in the bond price without actually participating in any objective-achieving projects. Hedgers wouldn't particularly want the value of their bonds to rise, but their bondholdings could similarly reduce the supply of bonds available to active investors.

None of these passive purchasers of Conflict Reduction Bonds would do much to help reduce violent political conflict. However, the way markets for the bonds would work to limit the scope for profitable passive investing. To see this, assume that would-be free riders succeed in buying a large proportion of the bonds in circulation. Then the bond issue as a whole would generate very little incentive for people to do anything to reduce conflict. So it is most likely that the targeted level of conflict would become more remote, and as it did so, so the value of all Conflict Reduction Bonds would fall. As the bonds lost value, they would become a more attractive purchase for people who *were* prepared actively to help achieve the targeted objective. So free riders would be tempted to sell, even at a loss, rather than see the value of their bonds continue to fall. Some history of falling Conflict Reduction Bond prices would tend to make free riding on the bonds less appealing with future issues. Free riding then would become a self-limiting activity.

There are other reasons why bondholding would be unattractive to potential free riders:

- Individual free riders would have no incentive to collude with other free riders, because the more they did so, the more remote the targeted reduction in conflict would become, and the further would the value of their bonds fall. This would act so as to limit any free riding activity to small players.

- As with other financial instruments, small players would have to pay higher transaction costs than the bigger institutions—the ones that would be most likely to initiate conflict-reducing projects.

- Small players also would not have access to all the research and information that would enable big players more accurately to value the bonds or anticipate their price movements. Therefore they would be at a disadvantage in the market.

Note also that even if free riders were to gain from holding Conflict Reduction Bonds, they would do be doing so only because their bonds had risen in value as a result of the targeted lower level of conflict becoming closer to being achieved As well, some attempted free riding would have important positive effects: it would add liquidity to the bond market, and increase the robustness of the market prices that would supply useful information to potential investors in the bonds.

In short, there are grounds to believe that free riding would not seriously undermine the operation of a Conflict Reduction Bond regime, mainly because it is unlikely much free riding would occur, and partly because even if it did occur it would not impede the operation of the bond mechanism.

# *FUTURES AND OPTIONS MARKETS*

Another possible source of perverse incentives could arise from the development of futures and options markets in Conflict Reduction Bonds. Certain derivatives when bought ('put' options for example) or sold would enable participants in futures and options market to benefit from a falling bond price, so giving them an incentive to delay achievement of the targeted reductions in conflict.

It is quite likely that there would be futures and options markets for large bond issues, and it is almost certain that the price of any particular Conflict Reduction Bond would not always be increasing along an upward trend from its float price to its redemption value. It would be justifiable, as well as efficient, if bondholders could hedge against consequent falls in the value of their assets. People who did not hold bonds might want to participate in markets for derivatives of bonds, some of which would rise in value as the targeted level of conflict became more remote. This in turn means that speculators and short sellers could certainly profit from short-term bond price falls, and the question is whether these people would then take steps to increase the level of conflict, and so impede progress towards the targeted objective.

There are two main reasons why they would probably not. The first is that, in the long term, the weight of money would be against them. Provided sufficient funds were allocated to achieving the targeted objective, there would be a net positive sum of money payable if the targeted reduction in conflict were to be achieved, and a net zero sum paid as long as the goal were not achieved. All the long-term incentive would be to achieve the targeted objective. Those who, for whatever reason, would suffer from achievement of the objective could be compensated by bondholders, or bribed to change their ideas. Note also that for every buyer of a 'put' option there would be a seller, and that for every futures contract bought on the expectation that the bond price would fall, there would be an equivalent futures contract sold on that basis, so that the net incentive generated by derivatives would be in line with the incentive created by the underlying financial instrument, the Conflict Reduction Bond: in the long run, this would favour achievement of the targeted objective.

The other reason that short sellers, or holders of 'put' options, in Conflict Reduction Bonds might not take actions aimed at interfering with achievement of the goal is that such actions might well already be illegal or, again given the incentives that the bonds would generate, be made illegal once the bonds had been issued. They would almost certainly be ethically objectionable as well. Derivatives that rise in value as the price of an underlying share falls are of course widely traded, and do not appear to generate any significant efforts aimed at undermining share prices.

Futures and options markets for Conflict Reduction Bonds would also make markets for Conflict Reduction Bonds more liquid, and so improve pricing efficiency.

## PERVERSE INCENTIVES

One potential disadvantage of Conflict Reduction Bonds is the possibility that bondholders could try to bring about peace in ways that conflict with other societal goals. It is hard to imagine much worse than war. But tyrannies and genocidal regimes can operate within their own borders; this raises two questions for a bond regime.

The first is whether Conflict Reduction Bonds could prevent regimes from killing or imprisoning their own population. What if violent regimes had been content to operate within their borders as was, say, Stalin's repressive regime, and, following the first Gulf War, that of Iraq's Saddam Hussein, or as North Korea's is today?

Could Conflict Reduction Bonds have discouraged the invasions that brought about an end to those regimes?

The second question is whether issuing Conflict Reduction Bonds might make oppressive regimes more secure, knowing that it would be in bondholders' interest not to provoke a conflict that would tend to lower the value of their bonds. Historical examples of where conflict has led to the downfall of dictatorships include World War II and the second Gulf War (2003). Few now dispute that, from the standpoint of 1939, the decision of Great Britain to go to war against Nazi Germany was morally justified. Nor that, in 1941, the US was right to go to war against Germany and Japan. If Conflict Reduction Bonds that targeted, say, the number of people killed in violent political conflict between states, had been issued then, they might have discouraged bondholders and their agents from waging war and this, we can assume, would have been against the interests of humanity.

The answer to these questions lies in the bonds' redemption terms. If Conflict Reduction Bonds are aimed at a particular conflict, its peace objective should not be limited to a reduction in the absolute numbers of people killed by armed violence in that conflict. Such a badly crafted objective could be achieved by, for instance, starving an entire population. Careful definition of bonds' target would solve this potential problem. It is an argument for including within the scope of a bonds target such elements as: numbers of people killed through violent political repression; numbers of men and women under arms; and military spending. Or the same concerns could be embodied in provisos that would have to be satisfied if the bonds were to be redeemed. Of course, for the bond mechanism to function well, information about the activities of societies such as North Korea would have to be sought, found and verified. But such information is more readily available today than in previous generations, and a bond regime would stimulate more interest. Merely seeking, accumulating and publicising information about, for example, North Korea's military, could serve extremely useful purposes in bringing the horrors of these regimes out into the open, and doing something to forestall them—quite independently of the direct incentives a bond regime would give to those opposing these regimes.

Proponents of Conflict Reduction Bonds might also argue that both Nazi Germany and the military Japan of the 1930s were regimes that had a history of war and conquest that preceded confrontation with the Allied Powers. Similarly for Saddam Hussein's Iraq, which had invaded Iran and Kuwait before western intervention. If bonds targeting conflict in the relevant parts of the world had been issued before these regimes had come into power, they or at least their military actions, would have met stronger opposition.

There is another source of potential perverse incentives, arising from the rises in market prices for Conflict Reduction Bonds when conflicts end. Governments or military organisations could experience windfall gains either from their own bondholdings, or from payments by bondholders, if they ceased engaging in armed conflict. So there would be a danger that these governments or organisations could cynically initiate or threaten to initiate conflict, buy bonds, then announce an end to the conflict and reap the rewards by selling the bonds at a higher price. A regime could threaten war, hoping then to buy up bonds that have consequently fallen in value; it could then moderate its rhetoric and sells its bonds for a higher price.

How could the potential for such a perverse activity be minimised? One response would be point out that preparation for war involves mobilisation of military personnel and materiel, which carries a cost. It also involves preparing public opinion,[88] and this takes time as well as money. The cynical government or military organisation then would have to invest considerable financial and political capital for a return from its bondholdings (or from bondholders) that might be large or small, but would definitely be uncertain. So, unless bondholders were exceptionally naïve, we could expect them to quickly distinguish between credible and unrealistic bellicose declarations.

The threatening party might also have cause to fear for its survival. Note that war can be defined as:

> "[A]n occurrence of purposive and lethal violence among two or more social groups pursuing conflicting political goals that results in fatalities, with at least one belligerent group organized under the command of authoritative leadership."[89]

It is the political nature of this conflict that distinguishes it from other forms of lethal violence such as mob lynchings, gang turf battles, and organized crime vendettas.[90] Politicians, even the most tyrannical, can be deposed. Politicians who declare aggressive intentions are more likely to be deposed if there is a bond regime that could finance opposition to them. Crucially, this holds *whether their declarations are genuine or not*. Bondholders would benefit by opposing or undermining a regime that threatened war. A regime thinking of threatening its neighbours would have to take this possibility into account, as well as the costs of believable preparations for war, when considering whether to make warlike noises.

Regime change would not be the worst fate that cynical warmongers might face from bondholders or their agents. Whoever declares war, or makes threats, is saying that they would be prepared to risk people's lives by creating conflicts. Bondholders would feel no ethical constraints, therefore, in putting such people in a position where they could no longer make such threats, again *whether such threats were cynical or not*. Whoever makes threats of this sort would, under a bond regime, be putting themselves at risk from bondholders who would be motivated to make sure that no such threats would be translated into action.

There are other considerations that further reduce the likelihood of perverse incentives leading to cynical behaviour:

- It would be in bondholders' long-term interest never to reward cynical aggressors. While it is possible to imagine particular instances when paying cynical warmongers would be effective, bondholders would be keen to avoid establishing a precedent. They might therefore nip any cynical behaviour in the bud by refusing to reward it even when their short-term interest might be to do otherwise. Cynical aggressors therefore would be most likely to succeed only if they bought bonds themselves while they were making aggressive noises. If their threats were unconvincing, they would pay a high price for their bonds, reducing the profitability of their pretence

- The most serious conflicts are the very large ones. As Lewis Fry Richardson found, World Wars I and II dominate the overall death toll over from about 1820 until 1950. Together they account for some 36 million deaths, or about 60 per cent of all the quarrel deaths in his 130-year study period.[91] The cynical aggressors are likely to threaten relatively small conflicts. If Conflict Reduction Bonds were aimed at building peace for large regions then the variation in bond price generated by the threats of small players would be dwarfed in comparison to the effects of the larger players. This would reduce any profits likely to accrue from cynical behaviour, even if it were successful.

Of course, another response to the problem posed by the possibility of cynical aggression is that such perverse incentives exist now. It is not far-fetched to imagine, say, the Chinese Government talking up tension between itself and Taiwan—having taken short positions in Hongkong or Taiwan shares—and then switching the rhetoric along with their portfolio holdings. And it is also true that

Egypt receives massive subventions from the US government that are conditional on its remaining at peace with Israel.

## DISCUSSION

The potential problems of a bond regime should not be overstated. Careful choice and specification of targeted objectives, combined with existing legal sanctions, would probably circumvent or remedy most of them. And we should not forget that the comparison that matters is with the current system, under which financial incentives to create conflict proliferate and are all too obviously exploited. Manufacturers of weapons or defence systems benefit from increased tension already, in obvious, financial ways. Conflict, or the fear of it, benefits all the executives, employees and shareholders of these companies. The overall effect of a Conflict Reduction Bond regime would act as a counterweight to such incentives.

In today's political environment policymakers and officials can escape or deflect censure because the adverse results of their policies are difficult to relate to their cause. If Conflict Reduction Bonds were to lead to negative effects, the relationship between these effects and their cause would be easier to identify, and deterring such effects would be simpler than doing so under the current activity- or institution-based funding arrangements.

# 6

# *Practical aspects of a Conflict Reduction Bond regime*

This chapter looks at some of the practical aspects of introducing and implementing a Conflict Reduction Bond regime.

## *INTRODUCTION OF A CONFLICT REDUCTION BOND REGIME*

Despite the high level of, and potential for, violent political conflict in today's world, there is some need to be cautious in introducing a new policy instrument targeted explicitly at conflict reduction. Governments and international organisations are bound to feel queasy at the prospect. But Conflict Reduction Bonds could first be tried out on an experimental basis. Initial goals could be relatively small scale and uncontroversial. They could be confined to a single conflict or region and could complement existing inter-governmental or United Nations programmes. There is one minor caveat, which applies to bonds targeting one particular conflict. That is that there should be little potential for the bonds to reduce that particular conflict *at the expense* of other conflicts. To dramatise this concern, assume that country X is threatening both country Y on its northern border and country Z on its southern border. The danger is that bonds targeting conflict between country X and Y could simply induce country X to transfer materiel to its southern border and inflame the conflict between itself and country Z. If that seemed likely, the best approach would be to expand the scope of the targeted conflict to include both borders.

Broadening the scope of targeted conflict would have another benefit: it would mean that returns, measured as conflict reduction per dollar outlay, will be higher. If the bonds target a wider range of conflicts, bondholders could choose those that will respond most readily to their efforts. In doing so they would maximise the reduction in worldwide levels of conflict per dollar outlay.

# PRIVATELY-BACKED CONFLICT REDUCTION BONDS

To be realistic, it is unlikely that the United Nations or governments will be the first to introduce a Conflict Reduction Bond regime. It has to be said that they are not renowned for innovative policy approaches. Fortunately, though national defence has been the stereotypical public good, that does not necessarily mean that governments or inter-governmental organisations can be the only backers of Conflict Reduction Bonds. Perhaps the way forward is for groups of NGOs or private individuals with a strong interest in a particular conflict, to back and issue their own Conflict Reduction Bonds, redeemable when that conflict had subsided or ended for a sustained period of time.

They could do this for a conflict that they would particularly like to see brought to an end, or one that they believe would most benefit from the sort of innovative projects that a bond regime might stimulate. It would not be too far-fetched, for example, for consortia to be formed of interested businesses or individuals issuing bonds aiming to reduce conflict in, for example, Northern Ireland or the Basque region of Spain where most people clearly wish to live in peace, and the numbers actively participating in political violence are probably very low.

Private backers could publicly launch their bond issue by depositing their donations into an escrow account. They could call for additional contributions to be deposited into that account by any other concerned people. (It would be helpful if such donations could be treated as charitable for tax purposes.) Bonds could be issued, and funds could continue to be added to the account. Each bond could be redeemable either for a fixed sum, or for a fixed proportion of the total amount in the escrow account once the conflict-reduction objective had been met. If the former, more bonds could be issued as more funds were deposited into the account. If the latter, there would be a fixed number of bonds issued, but their redemption value would increase as funds were deposited into the designated account.

At any time after issue then, Conflict Reduction Bonds could be traded, bondholders could be working to reduce conflict, and donations could be flowing into the escrow account. As well, any current conflict-reduction activities could continue. Existing conflict-reduction bodies might buy the bonds, which would give them a financial incentive to boost their conflict-reduction efforts.

Privately-backed Conflict Reduction Bonds could mobilise three groups of people:

- Ordinary, concerned members of the public, who could contribute to a fund that would be used to redeem the bonds. Many people already give donations to charities that help relieve some of the consequences of conflict. Contributions to a Conflict Reduction Bond fund would be similar, except that the donations would actually be paid out only once the specified conflict-reduction objective had been achieved. Before then, they could lie dormant in an interest-bearing escrow account.

- Wealthier, profit-motivated, companies or individuals, who could buy the bonds themselves, with the aim either of initiating conflict-reduction projects or of paying others to do so.

- People with time, energy, or ideas for peace-building, who could approach bondholders for financial support. Bondholders would be motivated to support those activities that looked likeliest to succeed.

Potential investors in Conflict Reduction Bonds would want more reassurance that their bonds will be redeemed if their bonds were backed by a private rather than public agency. Privately-backed bonds then would most probably be more successful if, before the bonds were issued, redemption funds were placed in an escrow account at a trusted institution. If such bonds were not redeemed because a targeted level of conflict were not reached, then the redemption funds would remain in the escrow account either indefinitely, or until a pre-determined time limit had elapsed, at which point they could be returned to their donors or given to a conventional charity.

# EXISTING INSTITUTIONS AND THE TRANSITION TO A CONFLICT REDUCTION BOND REGIME

If private sector bodies issued their own Conflict Reduction Bonds, they would most probably not have to contemplate reducing their support of existing bodies. But what about governments? There are many government and non-governmental agencies that do engage in conflict-reduction activities as part of their overall remit. There are also a number of bodies and NGOs researching into the causes of conflict, and rather more that are concerned with alleviating the impact of conflict on civilians. If they were to back Conflict Reduction Bonds, should they continue to fund existing bodies engaged explicitly or implicitly in conflict-reduction, and how should the transition to a bond regime be managed?

Currently neither these bodies, nor those that do have the explicit objective of minimising violent political conflict are being financially rewarded in ways that are correlated with their performance. Nevertheless these bodies have a great deal of expertise in building peace and some of them are bound to be efficient, or to be capable of becoming efficient, in doing so.

Depending on the exact specification of the outcomes targeted by Conflict Reduction Bonds, such bodies could expect to see an increase in their funding as a result of the introduction of a Conflict Reduction Bond regime, to the extent that they are cost-effective in reducing conflict or its adverse effects. It would be unwise as well as unfair and unnecessary if the funding of these bodies were cut too drastically at first. The answer would be a gradual weaning away from government funding. During the transition to a bond regime governments could continue to fund international bodies as well as peace research organisations and academic institutions at a decreasing rate; they could divert an increasing proportion of their total conflict-reduction support to a bond redemption fund, and let bondholders decide on how these funds should be allocated.

On introducing a bond regime governments could decide to reduce their funding of current conflict-reduction institutions by, say, 3 per cent a year, in real terms. (They could allocate the saved funding to the future redemption of the Conflict Reduction Bonds.) So after five years, each body would be receiving directly from governments only 85 per cent of the funding that it formerly received. But bondholders could choose to supplement the income of some of these bodies. They might, for instance, judge a particular agency of the United Nations to be especially effective at converting the funds they receive into measurable conflict-reduction benefits, as defined by their bonds' redemption terms. Particularly effective personnel may be working in deprived regions, where relatively small outlays could translate into large reductions in the potential for conflict. Or bondholders might judge a particular research body to be worthy of additional funding because it was conducting excellent research into the causes of conflict.

In all these cases bondholders would supplement government funding, and these favoured bodies might well end up receiving considerably more than their former income throughout the lifetime of a bond regime.

It is also very probable that bondholders would look at completely new ways of reducing conflict; ways that currently receive no, or very little, funding. To give a not entirely unbelievable example, bondholders might believe that one of the best ways of reducing conflict is to boost the political status of women in certain countries. Following this logic, bondholders might find that one of the most efficient ways of reducing conflict would be to add to the campaign funds of female candidates in some countries in the developing world. It is difficult to imagine how our current activity-or institution-based government fund allocation mechanisms could decide on such a programme.

Could bonds targeting a large reduction in conflict, such as a reduction in a worldwide Conflict Index by 50 per cent, be compatible with a gradual transition of the type described above, where funding to existing institutions reduces by 3 per cent annually? At first sight there would be an apparent mismatch between such incremental reductions in direct government funding and the time scale needed to reach such a long-range objective. The critical point here is that bondholders would be investing not on the basis of the annual reductions in government expenditure on existing conflict-reduction institutions, but on the basis of the redemption value of all the Conflict Reduction Bonds issued. To be more precise, it would be this total redemption value, minus the bonds' existing market value, that would inform bondholders' investment decisions. This sum could be many times each year's incremental reduction in government's institution-based spending. One of the virtues of a Conflict Reduction Bond regime is that even in the short term bondholders would begin to invest in projects with a long-range objective, on the expectation of capital gains that might arise only in the distant future.

Actually, it might be possible to expand spending allocated via the bonds at a faster rate. Once Conflict Reduction Bonds had shown their effectiveness, more resources might well be found for a succession of bond issues.

Amongst the first targets of a of a bond regime, whether backed by government or the private sector, could be those conflicts that are relatively small and self-contained, whose progress could be more easily measured. With such conflicts it would be a relatively simple matter to watch out for the sort of perverse behaviour described in the previous chapter. And once the bonds had gained acceptability amongst people in and out of government, more people could discuss and refine the bond concept and practical aspects of its implementation.

If the bonds at first targeted only incremental reductions in conflict, then observing and remedying any negative behaviour would be even simpler. Later tranches of bonds could incorporate provisos stipulating that they would be redeemed only if any unwanted, and previously untargeted, activities did not exceed a minimal level.

Those who back and issue bonds would collate and apply lessons learned from early trials to before launching bonds with wider application. Lessons could extend beyond how to deal with any perverse behaviour on the part of bondholders. They might, for instance, give some direction as to the circumstances under which bonds could best be used as complements to existing policies, and when they could safely replace them.

A cautious, gradual, introduction of Conflict Reduction Bonds would be one means of minimising potential problems of a bond regime. If, despite such an approach, bondholders behaved illegally, governments could prosecute the perpetrators. And if bondholders behaved in negative-but-legal, ways, government would have other options. In ascending order of severity, they could:

- Persuade or cajole bondholders into toeing the line. It could do this publicly or privately—initially, at least, holdings of Conflict Reduction Bonds could be registered in the same way as ownership of shares;

- Buy back bonds on the open market, which would have the effect of lowering the price of bonds remaining in circulation (by reducing the total redemption funds; see chapter 3); or

- Legislate against the negative activity.

If a government had issued the bonds it could, in extreme circumstances, even declare the bonds null and void, and offer compensation related to the bonds' issue price or their current market price.

## *INTERACTION WITH EXISTING PROGRAMMES AND PROJECTS*

In a transition to a Conflict Reduction Bond regime, government would directly supply a gradually declining proportion of funds. Those working in existing peace-building institutions might well respond by quickly reviewing how *all* their existing programmes and projects operate. On the one hand, the switch in the way funding is allocated would warn existing institutions that they could expect to see their relatively ineffective operations receive diminishing funds in the future. On the other hand, their effective operations could look forward to higher—possibly much higher—funding. Just as they would be subject to, say, 3 per cent annual cuts in funds from government sources, so they could expect to gain a proportion of funds spent by bondholders—provided they could show bondholders that they are cost-effective in translating funding into conflict-reduction. So a bond issue could bring about a rapid change in the way existing bodies conducted all their peace-building programmes. They may have to devote some time and energy into persuading potential investors in Conflict Reduction Bonds of the cost-effectiveness of their activities, but this would not represent a radical difference from the way they lobby for funding nowadays. Under a bond regime they would have to do their lobbying on a more transparent, outcome-oriented, basis. This could mean a refocusing of their efforts into areas where their activities would bring about greater benefits. It would almost certainly mean more information being gathered about conflict, its causes, consequences and remedies.

## *EFFECTS ON GOVERNMENT'S BEHAVIOUR*

One aspect of the integration of Conflict Reduction Bonds into the current policy-making system arises from governments' role as creators of statutes.

Government has the power to pass laws that would affect bond prices, or its actions could influence bond prices in other ways. For instance: governments in conflict areas could come under great pressure not to increase military spending from holders of Conflict Reduction Bonds (be they agencies within that government, or agencies of other governments, or private sector bodies). Note, though, that the source of the pressure, and the motivation for it, would be easy to identify. There would be nothing illegitimate about this: lobbying is a perfectly acceptable activity, and there is no reason why bondholders, in common with other pressure groups, should not lobby politicians. They would be doing so mainly out of financial self-interest of course: they would be lobbying for changes in government policy or legislation, and they would benefit in obvious, pecuniary, ways if they were successful. But existing pressure groups are also self-interested, and in the case of bondholders their self-interest would be both more transparent and more likely to coincide with society's interests, provided that targeted conflict-reduction objectives were correctly specified.

When they assess the value of the bonds, potential investors would take into account such possible changes in legislation and their potential influence on the speed at which the targeted objective could be achieved. Under a bond regime, would-be bondholders would want as much information about the behaviour of governments in targeted conflict regions as they could gather, and they might also try to influence these governments. People become wealthy by exerting influence on politicians under the current system, but they and their effects on behaviour are not always identifiable. As now, under a bond regime it would be up to politicians to weigh the evidence for and against any course of action promoted by lobbyists, with due regard to the lobbyists' motivation. And it would be up to potential investors in Conflict Reduction Bonds to take into account likely or possible changes in national or international legislation when bidding for the bonds.

The likelihood of bondholders' lobbying governments for legislative change could have a positive aspect. For bond issues to be as successful as possible, governments would ideally give assurances as to their future behaviour. These could mean making relatively simple decisions early on, or choosing to be more definite about their long-term spending plans.

Assume that a Conflict Reduction Bond had developed to such an extent that bonds targeting a worldwide Conflict Index had been issued. Then would-be bondholders would be very interested, for instance in certain governments' projected expenditure on the military, or on education, or peace research. Governments would maximise interest in the bonds by being as open about their legislative and spending intentions as soon as possible. Their assurances would doubtless be subject to the usual scepticism attending pronouncements of this type.

The question of government behaviour can be seen in a different light. Most governments, especially those contributing most to the bonds' redemption funds, as well as bondholders and society in general, would want Conflict Reduction Bonds to succeed. Or, which comes to the same thing, they would want to be seen to be wanting Conflict Reduction Bonds to succeed. Either way, their assurances about their legislative and spending plans will never be absolute but, by giving what assurances they could, governments would enhance the market for the bonds.

Of course, if the bonds were to target only small reductions in a Conflict Index governments' long-range plans would not be so significant to prospective bondholders. Targeting such incremental reductions could be the best way of dealing with uncertain future government behaviour. Markets routinely deal with uncertainty by attaching lower values to riskier instruments.

To safeguard against backers of Conflict Reduction Bonds reneging on their commitments to redeem the bonds they could be made to contribute funds intended to be used for bond redemption to the issuers, who would hold them in escrow. Of course, they would also be under strong moral pressure to comply with their commitment to redeem the bonds. But it would also be in the backers' own interest to fulfil their obligations. If they did not, they would be discrediting the entire bond principle, which they might well want to deploy again, either to continue to reduce violent political conflict or in to solve other global or national social and environmental problems.

## *ASSESSMENT OF INDICATORS AND INSIDER TRADING*

A bond regime would rely on authoritative, accurate and timely monitoring of the targeted components of a conflict so that progress towards their reduction could be impartially assessed. There would probably be private sector information gathering, but the definitive, official, figures would have to be seen to be independent of bondholders, who could benefit unfairly from dubious data collection. Naturally the information as to how close the objective were to being achieved would have value. It would not be difficult, for instance, to imagine the latest military budgets of large players being sought in advance of their official publication and used for 'insider trading' of Conflict Reduction Bonds that targeted a worldwide Conflict Index. If too much insider trading went on, it would increase the riskiness of the bonds to those without access to this information and tarnish their value as an investment. So how could it be minimised?

- Those involved in gathering, collating and processing relevant data could be bound by terms deterring or forbidding them from abusing privileged information.

- Indicators for the components of a Conflict Index could be chosen with a view to minimising the possibility of insider trading being an important factor. Some imprecision about exactly how some components were to be calculated could help: the bond issuers could, for example, target changes in military expenditure in a random sample of some African or Asian countries, rather than in all countries in these continents.

- The objective itself could be chosen to minimise the possibility of insider trading. Bonds targeting large reductions in a Conflict Index, such as 50 per cent, would probably be less sensitive to insider trading than bonds targeting only a 10 per cent reduction. With long-range objectives, each datum illegally withheld from the bond market would probably represent a smaller proportion of the total relevant information available to the bond market, and so have a lesser effect on the bond's market value.

None of these ways of mitigating insider trading would always be fully effective. That said, there are already sensitive indicators, such as US interest rates, or German unemployment or retail sales figures, that are capable of moving markets, and so there are already in place mechanisms to keep such information secret until it is time for publication. There are also sanctions against those who obtain, and act on, such information illegally. These mechanisms and sanctions might need to be strengthened under a bond regime, but it remains to be seen how important abuse of insider information would be. As well, there would most probably be a great deal of private information gathering: investors, bondholders, and financial commentators would take their own soundings throughout the lifetime of each bond issue. They would be interested in frequently updated information, so that progress toward conflict reduction could be readily charted. All this would serve to remove some of the allure from privileged figures that had yet to be publicised.

In short, while insider trading does mean that unscrupulous people benefit at the expense of the public, it does not generally impede the operation of markets, and the market for Conflict Reduction Bonds would be no exception.

## WHAT HAPPENS ONCE AN OBJECTIVE HAS BEEN ACHIEVED?

Assume that Conflict Reduction Bonds had been issued targeting a sustained reduction in a particular conflict, and that this objective were close to being achieved. What would happen then?

As the bonds were being redeemed, the issuing body could float a new set of bonds aimed at maintaining the achieved peace outcome, or at further reductions in the conflict level. Sustaining the outcome beyond the period specified in the original bond issue would most probably be cheaper than achieving it in the first place, while further improvements targeted by a second bond issue would be likely to cost less, in terms of conflict-reduction per unit outlay, than those achieved by the first issue. There are two linked reasons for this:

1. Bondholders may have invested in systems or capital assets that cost less, per unit conflict-reduction, to keep running than they did to set up.

2. Bondholders, in a similar fashion, would have learned from their experience of achieving the objective targeted by the first bond issue. They would have looked for, and experimented with, different methods of conflict-reduction and be able to choose the most efficient ones for subsequent bond issues. Any know-how about conflict avoidance or conflict reduction would be more cheaply available once an initial targeted lower level had already been achieved.

# 7

# *Market incentives to build peace*

Conflict Reduction Bonds would represent a radical shift in peace-building policy. They would be innovative in two main ways:

- by using market forces to achieve a societal goal, and
- by inextricably linking rewards to targeted outcomes, rather than institutions, programmes or activities.

By appealing to people's financial self-interest, Conflict Reduction Bonds could be more effective than conventional efforts aimed at reducing the level of violent political conflict. In channelling market forces into the achievement of this objective the bonds would ensure a maximum reduction in violence for the outlay of whoever contributes to the funds used to redeem the bonds.

Under a Conflict Reduction Bond regime, backers of the bonds, whether they be governments acting collectively or individually, NGOs or private individuals, would continue to set and rank conflict-reduction objectives. But they would surrender, within limits, their power to dictate *how* these objectives shall be achieved, and which institutions shall be charged with achieving them. Some politicians and official agencies might be reluctant to relinquish this power. And some of the beneficiaries of current policies might oppose a shift toward more transparent and effective conflict-reduction policies.

But for those genuinely seeking peace, these concerns need not be too worrying. In, the first place, the current regime is not strikingly successful. This is the standard against which any new approach must be compared, and it is a low standard. Violent political conflict, and the fear of it, are still rife in today's world. Current conflict-reduction activities, characterised as they are by centralised decision-making and an absence of a link between rewards and outcomes, have not been markedly successful in bringing about peace. The few who want to create and prolong conflict still threaten the many who wish for peace and stability. We do not know how efficient the current regime is in terms of conflict-reduction per unit outlay. In itself, that is a minor indictment of this regime. But we do know that the current regime has not brought peace to millions of innocent civilians. A new approach is at least worth trying.

A more positive reason for issuing Conflict Reduction Bonds is that they are versatile. At first, they could be used as supplements to existing conflict-reduction approaches. They can be tried first by the private sector, and at a relatively small scale. Thereafter the concept could be refined, extended, and taken up on a large scale by individual governments, and then by governments acting collectively.

In today's emotional climate decision-making is too often reactive. It is too easily swayed by media images that can distract attention from the more grievous conflicts that do not appear on television. Or decisions can be influenced by people with a propensity for violence or those who benefit from conflict, whether financially or emotionally. There are enlightened people and organisations working for peace, but their ability to raise and deploy resources effectively is constrained. The funding of the United Nations and other multilateral conflict-reduction bodies is conditional on their carrying out a range of activities limited by the imagination, insecurities and competence of their sponsoring governments. Private peace-building bodies work in admirable and diverse ways, but their efforts are relatively small-scale and uncoordinated. For both sets of organisations the financial rewards from reducing conflict are not correlated with their effectiveness in actually doing so. Conflict Reduction Bonds, in contrast, would explicitly reward movement towrd a targeted peace outcome. They would harness market efficiencies to the reduction of violent political conflict. They could be the most effective way of ushering in the era of world peace that humanity has so desperately wanted and needed for so long.

# *Epilogue*

Conflict Reduction Bonds are a particular application of the idea underlying Social Policy Bonds. That idea has been in the public domain since around 1988 and has not, to my knowledge, yet been adopted anywhere. But neither has it been dismissed outright. It tends to provoke initial enthusiasm amongst economists and decision makers, but then to be forgotten as other more pressing issues arise. Robert Shiller, Professor of Economics at Yale University, wrote to me at the end of 1996, praising the Social Policy Bond idea, saying that it creates "a large interest group for the solution of important problems. The political and other effects of creating such an interest group could be incalculable." A draft of my first book on the subject elicited extreme comments at both ends of the range from the two referees: one dismissed the text as an irrelevance. The other called the idea "original and ingenious" and "a substantial contribution to debate about public policy".

In April 2002, I presented a paper on the bond concept to joint meeting of the Agriculture and Environment Committees at the Organisation for Economic Cooperation and Development (OECD) in Paris. At the meeting, delegations from most of the OECD's member countries made comments on the paper. These were mostly along the lines of "this is very interesting—but unworkable in practice." But one of the delegates perhaps articulated the deeper feelings of those present, who were overwhelmingly government employees: "if this gets adopted we'll all be out of jobs!"

I am pleased though that, at the time of writing, certain private individuals have taken the initiative and are proposing to issue their own bonds, based on the Social Policy Bond idea. They are considering floating bonds for projects as diverse as boosting voter registration, raising literacy in developing countries and developing open-source software. Enthused by the bond concept, they are raising funds, or preparing to put up their own funds, to redeem bonds targeting objectives that they specify. I am heartened and encouraged by their efforts.

# Bibliography

*Investing for the future*, Ronnie Horesh, UK CEED Bulletin No 35, Centre for Economic and Environmental Development, Cambridge, UK, September-October 1991. (Presented as Room Document 3 to the December 1994 meeting of the OECD Joint Working Party of the Committee for Agriculture and the Environment Policy Committee.)

*Social Policy Bonds: Injecting market incentives into the solution of social problems*, Ronnie Horesh, AEU Occasional Papers, University of Cambridge, Cambridge, UK, August 1992.

*Injecting incentives into the solution of social problems: Social Policy Bonds*, Ronnie Horesh, Economic Affairs, vol 20 (3), Institute of Economic Affairs, London, September 2000.

*Better than Kyoto: how Climate Stability Bonds can inject market incentives into the achievement of a stable climate*, Ronnie Horesh, Writers Club Press, USA. ISBN: 0-595-21164-X, December 2001.

*Better than Kyoto: Climate Stability Bonds*, Ronnie Horesh, Economic Affairs, vol 22 (3), Institute of Economic Affairs, London, September 2002.

*Injecting incentives into the achievement of social and environmental outcomes: Social Policy Bonds*, Ronnie Horesh, iUniversity Press, Lincoln, Nebraska, USA. ISBN: 0-595-24823-3, 2002.

# *Websites*

http://socialgoals.com/ *Social Policy Bonds*: papers on various applications of the bond principle can be freely downloaded.

http://users.rcn.com/wware1/spb-game.html *SPB the game*: online simulation of Social Policy Bonds.

http://www.openknowledge.org/writing/open-source/scb/ *The Wall Street Performer Protocol.* Using Software Completion Bonds to fund open source software development.

# Endnotes

1. *Armed conflict as a public health problem,* Murray, C. J. L. et al, 'British Medical Journal' vol 324, pages 346-49, 9 February 2002.

2. *Civil wars kill and maim people-long after the shooting stops,* Ghobarah H., Huth P., Russett B. (Draft 29 Aug 2001). Center for Basic Research in the Social Sciences. One statistical assessment, based on a cross sectional analysis, indicates that the total disability-adjusted life years lost in 1999 owing to the indirect effects of military conflicts occurring between 1991 and 1997 was about the same as the number lost owing to the direct effects of all wars in 1999.

3. Saferworld, UK http://saferworld.org.uk.

4. *World Report on Violence and Health,* World Health Organization, September 2002.

5. For a list of compilations of violent conflicts, see *Violent Conflicts 1400 A.D. to the Present in Different Regions of the World,* Peter Brecke, The Sam Nunn School of International Affairs, Georgia Institute of Technology Atlanta, GA, United States, http://www.inta.gatech.edu/peter.html.

6. Saferworld, UK http://saferworld.org.uk

7. Saferworld, UK http://saferworld.org.uk

8. *The horror of land mines,* Gino Strada, 'Scientific American', May 1996 (pages 40-45).

9. *Mortality associated with use of weapons in armed conflicts, wartime atrocities, and civilian mass shootings: literature review.* Coupland R. M., Meddings D. R., 'British Medical Journal' vol 319, pages 407-10 (1999). "The overall impact of these health effects is likely to be substantial. The reported ratio of people injured to those killed in modern conflicts ranges from 1.9 to 13.0."

10. *The global burden of disease,* Murray C. J. L., Lopez A. D., Harvard University Press, 1996. "In 1990 the *Global Burden of Disease* study estimated

that non-fatal outcomes of war resulted in 4.8 million disability adjusted life years worldwide, about the same as fires and more than half that caused by road traffic injuries."

11. *Peoples versus states*, Ted Robert Gurr, United States Institute of Peace Press (chapter 2), 2000.

12. *World refugee survey*, published annually by the United States Committee for Refugees.

13. *Peace and conflict 2001: a global survey of armed conflicts, self-determination movements, and democracy* Gurr T. R., Marshall M. G., Khosla, D., Center for International Development and Conflict Management, University of Maryland, 2001.

14. *Peace and conflict 2001*, op cit note 13.

15. *Global conflict trends*, http://members.aol.com/CSPmgm/conflict.htm webpage maintained by Center for Systemic Peace, Policy IV project, dated 20 September 2000, sighted 21 August 2003.

16. *Peoples versus states*, op cit note 11 (chapter 6).

17. *Peace and conflict 2001*, op cit note 13.

18. *Global conflict trends*, op cit note 15.

19. *The horror of land mines*, Gino Strada, 'Scientific American', May 1996 (pages 40-45).

20. *SIPRI Yearbook 2002*, Stockholm International Peace Research Institute, June 2002.

21. *Roll back malaria*, WHO Factsheet, http://www.rbm.who.int (sighted April 2003).

22. *Blood rites: origins and history of the passions of war*, Barbara Ehrenreich, Virago Press (pages 239-40), 1998.

23. *Sharing best practices on conflict prevention: the UN, regional and subregional organizations, national and local actors*, Report of a workshop held by the International Peace Academy and the Swedish Institute in Alexandria, Egypt, 8-10 April 2002.

24. 'The conviction that any one group has exclusive possession of truth and goodness is a root cause of prejudice and boundaries that allow for dis-

crimination and worse.' Oliver McTernan, *War Cries*, 'the Times', 12 August 2003.

25. *From reaction to conflict prevention*, Fen Osler Hampson and David M. Malone, editors, Boulder: Lynne Rienner, 2002.

26. *The cycle of violence*, Cathy Widom, 'Science', vol 244, pages 160-66, 1989.

27. *The global menace of local strife*, 'The Economist , 24 May 2003 (page 26).

28. *The economics of war: the intersection of need, creed and greed*, Conference Report, Woodrow Wilson International Center for Scholars, Washington, D.C. 10 September, 2001.

29. Elizabeth Picard of the Institut de Recherche et d'Etudes sur le Monde Arabe et Méditerranéan, speaking at: *The economics of war: the intersection of need, creed and greed*, Conference Report, Woodrow Wilson International Center for Scholars, Washington, D.C. 10 September, 2001.

30. *Statistics of deadly quarrels*, Richardson, Lewis F. Edited by Quincy Wright and C. C. Lienau. Pittsburgh: Boxwood Press, 1960.

31. Ibid.

32. Ibid.

33. *War and peace*, Leo Tolstoy (translated by Ann Dunnigan), New York: Signet Classic, 1968 (page 730).

34. Much of this section originates in *Post-Cold War opportunity and challenge*, 'Conflict prevention: a guide', Conflict Prevention Web, Creative Associates International.

35. *Post-Cold war opportunity and challenge*, op cit note 34.

36. *Sharing best practices on conflict prevention*, op cit note 23.

37. SIPRI Yearbook 2002, Stockholm International Peace Research Institute, June 2002.

38. *Post-Cold War Opportunity and Challenge*, op cit note 34.

39. Ibid.

40. Ibid.

41. *Economic growth, civil wars, and spatial spillovers*, Murdoch, James C. and Sandler T., Paper prepared for the Conference on 'Data Collection on Armed Conflict', Uppsala, Sweden, 8-9 June 2001.

42. *2001 Report: Criteria to authorise or refuse arms exports*, Romeva, R. Paper prepared for the Conference on 'Data Collection on Armed Conflict', Uppsala, 8-9 June 2001.

43. John Kay, 'Financial Times', 8 May 2003.

44. *Why states believe foolish ideas: non-self-evaluation by states and societies*, Stephen Van Evera, Massachusetts Institute of Technology, Political Science, Department and Security Studies Program, 10 January, 2002.

45. Source: OECD.

46. See, for example, *Perverse incentives: subsidies and sustainable development*, de Moor A. P. G., Institute for Research on Public Expenditure, The Netherlands, 1996.

47. *Distributional effects of agricultural support in selected OECD countries*, OECD, 1999.

48. See *Agricultural policies in OECD countries: monitoring and evaluation*, OECD. Published annually.

49. *Privatising peacemaking*, Doug Brooks, Bradlow Fellow, South Africa Institute of International Affairs, in conversation with Stephen Mbogo of 'West Africa', 18 September 2000.

50. *Privatising peacemaking*, op cit note 50.

51. *SIPRI Yearbook 2002*, Stockholm International Peace Research Institute, June 2002.

52. *The Military Balance 2000/2001*, International Institute for Strategic Studies, October 2000.

53. *United Nations peacekeeping: Questions and answers.* http://www.un.organisation/Depts/dpko/dpko/ques.htm, sighted 22 May 2003.

54. *Security with a human face: a proposal to create a Human Security Report*, web page prepared by Andy Mack following 'Euroconference' on 'Identifying Wars: Systematic Conflict Research and its Utility in Conflict Prevention and Resolution', Uppsala, Sweden, 8-9 June 2001.

55. *Assessing the societal and systemic impact of warfare*, Monty G. Marshall, in, 'From Reaction to Prevention: Opportunities for the UN System in the New Millennium', edited by David Malone and Fen Osler Hampson, International Peace Academy. Lynne Rienner Publishers, 2001.

56. *Making the world safe for politicians*, Harry Browne, http://www.harrybrowne2000.org/text/safe.htm (dated 22 February 1998, sighted 20 August 2003).

57. *The balance sheet*, John Kay, 'Prospect', UK, July 2002.

58. Ibid.

59. Dr Jonathan Michie, Lecturer at the Judge Institute of Management Studies, and Fellow of Robinson College, Cambridge, UK, speaking at a seminar on *The elusive concept of sovereignty*, held at the Finnish Institute in April 1996.

60. *The spirit of reform: managing the New Zealand state sector in a time of change*, Allen Schick. State Services Commission, Wellington, 1996.

61. Government Performance and Results Act of 1993.

62. *Guide to assessing agency annual performance plans*, General Accounting Office of the USA (1997), (http://www.gao.gov/special.pubs).

63. *The evaluation of economic policy*, Robin Johnson; paper prepared for annual conference of the New Zealand Association of Economists, Auckland, 25-27 June 2003.

64. *Looping the loop: evaluating outcomes and other risky feats*, and *Essential ingredients: improving the quality of policy advice*, State Services Commission, New Zealand, 1999.

65. *The Social Development Approach*, Proctor, R.. and *An inclusive economy*, Rea, D., papers presented at the Institute of Policy Studies, Wellington, New Zealand, 21 August 2001.

66. *Evidence-based policy and practice in social policy*, Rea D., Institute of Policy Studies, Wellington, New Zealand. Newsletter 70, August 2002.

67. *Death by evaluation? Reflections on monitoring and evaluation in Australia and New Zealand*, Ryan, B., Conference on Public Sector Performance (organised by Business Information in Action), Wellington, New Zealand, 17 October 2001.

68. *The evaluation of economic policy,* op cit note 64. The author is discussing the work of Ryan (note 68).

69. *Armed conflict as a public health problem,* op cit note 1.

70. *An agenda for democratization,* Peter Boutros Boutros-Ghali, New York, United Nations, 1996.

71. *Responding to terrorism: what role for the United Nations?* International Peace Academy, report of a conference held on 25-26 October 2002, New York.

72. *A Framework for lasting Disarmament, Demobilization, and Reintegration of former combatants in crisis situations,* IPA-UNDP Workshop Report, 12-13 December 2002, New York.

73. Ibid.

74. *The economics of war: the intersection of need, creed and greed,* Conference Report, Woodrow Wilson International Center for Scholars, Washington, D.C. 10 September, 2001.

75. *Statistics of deadly quarrels,* Brian Hayes, 'Computing Science', January-February 2002.

76. *The thinkable,* op cit note 43.

77. Ibid.

78. *The nuclear axis of evil,* Michael Ledeen, nationalreviewonline (http://www. nationalreview.com), 2 May 2003.

79. *Data issues in the study of conflict,* Paul Collier and Anke Hoeffler, Paper prepared for the Conference on 'Data Collection on Armed Conflict', Uppsala, Sweden, 8-9 June 2001.

80. Ibid.

81. *Getting to war: predicting international conflict with mass media indicators,* W. Ben Hunt, University of Michigan Press, 1997.

82. See the Center for Systemic Peace web page: http://members.aol.com/csp-mgm/warcode.htm.

83. *Notes on developing a Human Security/Insecurity Index,* Peter Brecke, Sam Nunn School of International Affairs, Georgia Institute of Technology, United States, 28 May 2002.

84. *Africa: the heart of the matter*, 'The Economist', 13 May 2000.

85. *Why states believe foolish ideas: non-self-evaluation by states and societies*, Stephen Van Evera, Massachusetts Institute of Technology, Political Science, Department and Security Studies Program, 10 January, 2002.

86. *The global menace of local strife*, The Economist, 24 May 2003 (page 25).

87. See Hayek, F. A., 'The Pretence of Knowledge', in his *New Studies in Philosophy, Politics, Economics and the History of Ideas*, University of Chicago Press, Chicago, 1978

88. *Getting to war: Predicting international conflict with mass media indicators*, op cit note 82.

89. *Origins and evolution of war and politics*, Cioffi-Revilla, Claudio, International Studies Quarterly, vol 40 (1), pages 1-22 (March 1996).

90. *Violent conflicts 1400 A.D. to the present in different regions of the world*, Peter Brecke, Sam Nunn School of International Affairs, Georgia Institute of Technology, Atlanta, United States. Paper prepared for the 1999 Meeting of the Peace Science Society (International) on 8-10 October 1999 in Ann Arbor, Michigan, United States.

91. *Statistics of Deadly Quarrels*, op cit note 30.

0-595-29484-7